KENTUCKY
a state of mind

Nov 10, 2005

David Dick

DAVID DICK

AND

LALIE DICK

Lalie Dick

ILLUSTRATIONS BY JACKIE LARKINS

First Edition, November, 2005

Copyright by
Plum Lick Publishing, Incorporated
P. O. Box 68
North Middletown, KY   40357-0068
or
1101 Plum Lick Road
Paris, KY 40361

www.kyauthors.com

Dust jacket design and book production
by Stacey Freibert Design

Back inset photo by Chuck Perry

Illustrations by Jackie Larkins

Other books by David Dick

The View from Plum Lick
Peace at the Center
A Conversation with Peter P. Pence
The Quiet Kentuckians
The Scourges of Heaven
Follow the Storm: A Long Way Home
Jesse Stuart – The Heritage

Other books by David and Lalie Dick

Home Sweet Kentucky
Rivers of Kentucky

ISBN: 0-9755037-1-5

Library of Congress Control Number
2005907715

In memory of

Dr. Thomas D. Clark

Historian Laureate of Kentucky

CONTENTS

PART *One*

PART *Two*

CONTENTS

PART *Three*

PART
One

Yesterday is gone and what is past is past.

Tomorrow isn't here yet

so we can't do anything about that until it's here.

What matters most of all is now.

Coming Home

$\mathcal{O}$ne of the best things about living in Kentucky is the coming back after being gone for a while. When we turn in at the front gate, past the twin plum trees, through the row of blooming Bradford pears, toward the ancient water maples, we know in our bones, we've done the right thing.

We shouldn't be living anyplace else. This is where we belong—with the grassroots people.

This is homeland—a state of mind—which, of course, is possible in any land at any time. Yet, Kentucky is quietly out of the ordinary, providing a common ground encouraging human beings to reach within themselves and be themselves in the way Kahlil Gibran described "beauty" in *The Prophet:*

Beauty is eternity gazing at itself in a mirror.

But you are eternity and you are the mirror.

Eternity in Kentucky is the movement of the Great Water Cycle. The mirror refracts in the cloud formations, the droplets coming to rest on blowing blades of bluegrass. Most Kentuckians live intimately in this eternity—clouds, sun, and the moisture.

There is no death.

Imagine, then, *Kentucky—A State of Mind* is an abiding closeness, an assembly of consciousness with nature and creatures of many kinds.

There's no mistaking home. The dogs come out to greet with licks and tail quivers. If Kink, Pumpkin, and Duff could talk they wouldn't say, "What did you bring us other than yourself?" If the walls of the mudroom could speak, they might say, "Come on in here, prop up your feet, and tell us a little, but not too much about the trip."

We let our fingers fold the pages of the road map before filing it away on the memory shelf along with several new books discovered along the way.

The journey to southern Florida—along the Gold Coast from Coral Gables to Palm Beach, a short stay in a high-rise hotel on the water's edge at Fort Lauderdale where the luxury yachts pant at their moorings, a stop at Port St. Lucie, northward to Cocoa Beach—became a lesson in the dubious accumulation of artificial wealth.

How much does a human being really need?

We came through a hard, swirling rain spawned by another season of hurricanes and tropical storms, warning enough that we ought to be going home to Kentucky where our greater need was firewood and three-dog nights.

Multimillion-dollar condo complexes stood vacant awaiting the annual arrival of snowbirds from as far away as the Yukon. We knew we had neither the conviction nor the wherewithal to be in their feathered company.

We called to mind the first sight of the mountains of Whitley County as we came up I-75 along Hell's Point Ridge past Jellico, then along Clear Fork of Cumberland River, the haze beginning to take on an unmistakable Kentucky hue. Made us want to roll the window down and breathe deeply!

There's much to do in our winter of content—appreciation of small treasures, the return to simple values, the building of a finer community. We need neither mega-yachts nor rapid transit authorities.

We need quiet time and, maybe, a good book or two to bring us safely and truly home.

If we were to retreat to Florida in winter and Canada in summer, it would be like celebrating a birthday without cake and candles. It would be like a pucker without the kiss, flicker without wisp of breath, Camelot without Richard Burton and Julie Andrews.

Let us gather ourselves beneath the magnolia tree—oh no, let us not stray far from there. Let us be the new green coming on. Let us simply BE.

Let us live in Kentucky, a state of mind, in every season, through every storm, through every calm moment, sunrise to sunset.

Storehouse of Ideas

Rain began falling softly, then steadily in the early morning on the tin roof of our mortal selves.

It was the old familiar—sometimes troubling, sometimes reassuring—pattern of sound. We lay in bed, and we quietly listened for messages. We were expectant not of voice mail, but of ideas arriving internally.

Flush in the joy of the birth of our new book *Rivers of Kentucky*, we knew instinctively there's hardly anything more pleasant and important as a new idea, or an old idea freshly inspired by falling rain.

We recalled the homeland along the miles of the banks of the Mississippi River from Wickliffe to Hickman, then around the circling Kentucky Bend, where people—farmers, welders, electricians, shopkeepers, clerks, retirees, teachers, students, doctors, nurses, lawyers, towboat crews, fishermen and descendants of Indian chiefs—stir and arise on another new day.

As for Ol' Man River, he plays no favorites. The wise (or shall we say, the river-rat savvy) respect the power of the Great Stream, because it flows no matter our attitude or mood, whether we're good or bad. The water responds to Ol' Man Gravity, and we surely know all about *his* reality. Without the absolute mandate of Mr. Gravity we'd be poured in a watery second into the great big bucket of space.

Then, where'd we be?

In the month of March, with enough high water, up and down crests, and windblown surprises to keep us fully employed for another century or two, it might be as good a time as any to put on waterproof shoes, take stock, and try a little of Grandmother's annual remedy. She'd open up the windows, air out the house, and lay in a new bottle of spring tonic.

There are enough litter, debris, and cobwebs from excessive holidays past lying all around us, stuff just aching and daring to be pitched. Might even be time for a fresh coat of paint or an occasion for considering an untried garden seed.

During the winter past, we had the good fortune to stumble upon a book, *Self-Made in America: Plain Talk for Plain People about the Meaning of Success*, by John McCormack. When it was published fourteen years ago, the price was $19.95, but Book Warehouse downstream in Baton Rouge had it marked down to ninety-nine cents—and we couldn't resist that kind of bargain! A storehouse of ideas, we brought the volume back to Plum Lick Creek in Kentucky to help keep us warmer and drier on rainy, windy March mornings.

The idea is to dare to dream, put well thought-out plans into action, stay focused, go with the flow of earthly and spiritual life, and don't ever lose sight of a worthy harbor. In short, don't give up, and whatever we do, keep our heads above muddy water. Otherwise, we might as well be driftwood and be done with it.

Determined, ethical work is everybody's improved state of mind. The village and the nation are built on individual excellence, commitment, and persistence.

It begins at home port.

It flows to the workplace.

Dedicated effort and pride in workmanship are master oar strokes to success in the finest meaning of the word.

As we move closer to another graduation season, when more young deckhands tie on their new career stanchions for holding power, it's not too late to examine and re-examine the quality of main-deck preparation. It might be learned at a school board meeting, a parent-teacher conference, a parent-student reality check, or in those pre-dawn moments with an early morning rain falling gently down.

It might even begin with a little ninety-nine cent book washed ashore by Ol' Man River.

Beginnings

The great water doctor moves in mysterious ways, sometimes like a whisper on the wind, rattling the windowpanes of the soul.

Perfectly round moisture droplets roll down the roof of this place we call home. The watering of the jonquils finished, the grass turned green from sleep, the fertile bottom pasture becomes a wetland of summer promise.

An unmistakable inner voice is heard:

"Go check to see where Plum Lick Creek begins."

"Doesn't it begin in a spring up the holler where Plum Lick road makes its first turn to the north? You know, back up there where deer cross in pairs, sometimes in fours or more? Down a skip and jump from the rocks where the old tollhouse used to stand, sentineled for passage of horse-drawn wagons on the way to market?"

"Don't be too sure."

"I'd not dare to do so, but what are you trying to tell me?"

"Not a case of trying. I am pointing in a direction you seem to have missed."

"I'm listening."

"Do you happen to remember the deadend road leading from the village where you spent your growing years?"

"Yes."

"Well, drive out there, go 3.1 miles to the edge where the paved road stops, get out, walk to the boundary, and look."

It didn't seem possible that such a little road had so many old trees, gatherings of water for sunfish and tadpoles, new homes, freshly painted church, small well-tended cemetery—views as valid as any on Earth.

"You see how much you've missed? Right at your very feet? Yours to touch and taste? Yours to see and feel. And listen!"

In the mind's eye, it becomes clearer—Plum Lick Creek begins in myriad places—tens of thousands of harboring pools, each one a likely place to anchor hope.

Coming back up one of the last hills, a young man stands near the place he calls home. The inner voice suggests stopping and speaking, to ask about headwaters.

The young man walks over to greet the visitor, and the conversation sets the tone for a well-saved late winter day.

All I want to know is exactly where Plum Lick Creek begins. All he wants me to know is that a doctor once told him, he, "the patient," had eight months to live.

Now, here was the "sufferer" leaning on the edge of the car's rolled down window, smile on his face, talking about his malignancy, which he was so pleased to say, had dried up. Well, you might say, as much as anybody had a right to expect. Maybe enough for another ten years of watching winters turn to springs, building houses as a trade, minding a son growing as fast as a well-watered weed.

There was an excitement written all over the young man's face as he told the story of hearing the doctor's terminal words, then going home to pray, to read, to learn, to investigate. The "victim" wrote letters, reached out to other doctors on knife-edged, advancing technologies. Day by day, year by year, there were new moments filled with brighter expectation.

It was as if a wanderer had gone looking for a simple source of water and instead had found a fellow creek walker, an inspired man who places a higher, dedicated value on his sojourning life and had decided to defy one doctor's professional but flawed opinion.

Of course, there are no guarantees, no ironclad agreement that there'll always be another season of sweet beds of mint alongside each creek bend. Yet, it seems reasonable to look for ways to take better charge of one's own flowing destiny.

Ease up.

Slow down.

Unwind.

We retrace our steps downstream, looking for small satisfactions — a sidestep for plumb ornery creatures, a smile for mankind making do with tools at hand.

For example, when the garbage man stops in the early morning darkness, it's good to hear his voice when a helping hand is extended.

We don't know his name. What counts is another safe passage of all those following Plum Lick Creek.

"Thanks, Buddy," he says.

And we say, "See you next time."

Connections

Beginnings seem to imply endings, but we choose to cast our lot with eternity. Therefore, the "next times" can be counted on.

But, the road will not always be smooth. Plum Lick Creek will writhe from flash flood to bone dry. And our love here in the valley will erode from passionate outpourings to tinderbox dry.

Thunder and lightning will leave creatures wild-eyed and wondering. From Kentucky Bend in the west to Big Sandy in the east, there'll be pop-ups to remind us that weather is The Great Equalizer.

Today's mild breeze becomes tomorrow's torrid blast—there's nothing that can change the reality of storm systems. They may sometimes seem to be signaling the end of the world, but after the clashes have moved through, there's the better prospect of quiet relief.

There's a music in the weather, a grand composition ever changing.

Kentuckians revel and rejoice in it.

They understand it.

Some call it "hip bone connected to the thigh bone." Kipling called it "Predestination in the stride o' yon connectin'-rod."

Old friends call it dominoes falling.

The summer of 2000 included a series of storms that began with a piano player and ended with plenty of wood for the fireplace.

Our neighbors, Michael and Miranda, invited us to come over and listen to Freddie George, a pianist from Louisville. Freddie understands pure pitch as well as a thunder baby knows its mama.

We sat out by a little lake and heard "Prisoner of Love," "Danny Boy," "Harbor Lights"—old songs from the time when we kissy-faced in the moonlight. That was back when thunder and lightning were mainly sound effects for passions galore.

But, on this evening, there were serious, take-no-prisoners rumblings rushing out of the southeast. The wind began to blow the willows over into the water. The tied canoes bobbed up and down. Thunder tromped the blackened sky and lightning turned crazier than anything we'd ever seen in Texas (the place where lightning is believed to have been invented).

The piano player retreated inside, and we decided it was time to tuck tail and head home. Driving down Plum Lick Road was as skeery as Shelley's "Angels of rain and lightning." Wind had collapsed a neighbor's greenhouse and taken the roof off his shed.

As we approached our house, where the storm-smart water maples are more than eighty years old, one of the trees had snapped about eight feet up and crashed through the fence. A wind shear had uprooted another ancient maple patriarch and heaved it lengthwise in front of the house, ripping out the gutter, missing the porch by inches.

We stood in the rain, gaped, and cursed.

"Damn it."

"Just damn it to Hell and gone, anyway."

"Now don't get riled. The Lord giveth, the Lord taketh away."

"What's the Lord got against innocent old water maples?"

"Why don't he go to Georgia and pick on pine trees?" Easier work.

Next morning, we took the chain saw and had it sharpened. Bought a sledgehammer and rounded up the steel wedges. Now, we've got enough firewood for thirty winters.

A little gift from the Almighty? Maybe so.

We heard an incessant hum, then noticed a peculiar stain on the trunk of the first tree. Beehive. So, we called a beekeeper, and he came out and removed a fine colony of bees. He promised to return next year with a new queen and several hives to help pollinate our clover field.

Called the gutter man, and he fixed that problem while our family discussed woolly worms and came up wooling with the usual quandary about whether this'll be a "good" or a "bad" winter. City folks generally prefer "good" winters, because they speed up getting to and from work. Farm folks are usually partial to "bad" winters, because it conditions the soil and cuts back on the insect population.

One of the steel wedges said, "Hit me square, or don't hit me at all," and left a razor-sharp sliver as a reminder that it was serious.

The chain saw said "I've had about enough of this," tightened up and refused to make one more cut.

Found a small engine repairman, Mousie Crouch, on the other side of Sharpsburg, and he performed brain surgery on the chain saw. While the patient rested in the recovery room, the doctor took us into his house and played a tune on his banjo.

Then he played the fiddle.

Then the guitar.

The doctor's wife played a hymn on the electric organ.

Our feet woke up, and we were smiling from ear to ear. Praise the Lord.

Man shows up on our doorstep and wants to know if we have any trees we'd like to have "harvested." We say, "How 'bout a couple of water maples?"

He smiled, but he was in more of a black walnut and wild cherry state of mind. On any other day we would have probably said, no, we love our trees and they love us. Instead, we said, let's go look. He spotted about a dozen and said he'd be back to get them. This may offend purists but why wait until lightning strikes and the wind begins to blow?

Somebody, somewhere will never know the origin of a new piece of furniture or, maybe, the front door to a house.

Listen!

It all began with that piano player from Louisville, "Stardust," Mousie Crouch, and a strong wind out of the southeast.

Jess

Jess Wilson is at home on Possum Trot Road in northwestern Clay County, just over the county line from Egypt, High Knob, Gray Hawk, and Swindling Gap in Jackson County.

Jess uses more brainpower than a lot of people we know. His mind works constantly, always trying to figure out how something ticks. He sees something living inside a piece of wood and out it comes. The first thing he does each morning is to write a paragraph or two, because he's a journal-keeping mountain man.

Jess, 87 years old, and Ruth, 86, married when they were 21. Since then, it's been 65 years of, shall we say, learning through sharing knowledge with themselves and others.

Since this is the early part of another school year, the ideas of Possum Trot Road can be a signpost for education outside as well as inside the classroom.

Ruth is a retired teacher, and Jess is retired from a long career with the local rural electric cooperative. Much younger than their years might suggest, Jess and Ruth haven't stopped learning.

No, Buddy!

A visit with them is like peeping into a time capsule, putting a stethoscope to faded pages of letters, and being more than a little curious about the wonders of pre-history.

"Put your finger here on this stone table and know that you are touching a form of life that was here long before human beings and dinosaurs," says Jess, a passionate collector with an insatiable appetite for understanding and preservation. Yet, he's anything but a purist. Everything has a purpose in the grand design of creation.

For Jess and Ruth, absolute time is hard to pin down or put into a bottle. Life is an unending time of search and discovery. Winter is as certain as death. Spring is as sure as resurrection. Summer is a gardener's delight. Autumn is the time of reflection.

"I've gone to find myself. If I get back before I return, keep me here," says the sign on the door of Jess's six-sided Battle Abbey (named for William the Conqueror's victory at the Battle of Hastings, in 1066).

Jess Wilson's Battle Abbey is a Kentuckian's last stand for truth— shelves for religion, non-secular volumes, and boxes, boxes, boxes of open-file records. Jess is a genealogist for people in forty-six states and several foreign countries.

No file clerk—just Jess Wilson.

Then there's "The Wigwam," which Jess and Ruth built up on one of the forested hills of their three hundred acres—a secluded clearing where family, friends, and others can gather to celebrate a wedding with one hundred guests, a New Year's celebration, or just to kick back and chill out. The Wigwam has multiple bunks and a heating apparatus built with three 55-gallon drums stacked one on top of the other in order to spread more evenly the warmth on cold, blustery nights.

Jess says, "Family reunions are best when they're held on neutral ground—no varnish or paint on anything, which helps to save the unvarnished truth and discourage the cosmetically superficial, bane of Everyman's existence—just the basics, an improved infrastructure for well-intended humankind.

One of Jess Wilson's prides is his Possum Trot University Press, the ultimate in self-publishing audacity. One of his titles—*The Sugar Pond and The Fritter Tree*—includes stories about "Shaving with Grandma's Razor" and "Working College Algebra." Jess has a way of making learning a fun thing to do.

Then there's Jess's tribute to the noble mule, "Thou Shalt Not Covet a Good Team of Mules:"

> *Perhaps some day, the clouds will roll back, the thunder will roar and a voice from the sky will proclaim, 'Jess, your time is up, your work is done. However, we are giving you one more year to find the contentment and peace you have been searching for,' then I would, most assuredly, go over to buy Cousin's Bill's mules or ask for the loan of them anyway.*

Jess has written "A Forest Benediction."

> *May we grow in spirit*
>   *as tall as a pine tree,*
>
> *And be in character*
>   *as sturdy as an oak.*
>
> *May our fortitude be*
>   *to the storms of adversity*
>   *as a willow in the wind.*
>
> *May our generosity be as free*
>   *as the shade of a maple*
>   *on a hot summer's day.*
>
> *And our reverence be*
>   *as prayerful as a spruce*
>   *in winter's snow."*

17

Trees As Teachers

Not until well past three score and ten did we begin to think of trees as teachers.

Each day now, reaching for another branch of maturity, the first thing we see from our window to the west is the ambitious green ash growing and claiming its share of the sky. We planted it there as a sapling in honor of the Prathers, one of the stalwart Plum Lick families who've lived here before us. Their descendants have been coming back for reunions, finding shade and soft breezes blowing through.

"Wouldn't trade this for a million dollars."

"This is the room where I was born."

"This is the room where Granddaddy was laid out."

"Here's where the log part used to be."

"See this big, black spot on the floor? It's where I started a fire one time. Don't know why. Just did it. Wonder the house didn't burn down."

From the rocking chair on the front porch, the view to the north includes the sprig that decided entirely on its own that it would take the place of the octogenarian water maple. It had withstood many a storm until the one that brought it down inches from the corner of the house where so many children have been born and so many matriarchs and patriarchs have been honored in death. The sapling knows only youthful thoughts, which is good.

On the northern side too is the new purple plum tree replacing the cedar where the eight Prather boys climbed and posed on stobs for a once-in-a-lifetime picture to be taken. The purple plum has a fragment and fragrance of memory. The Prather boys will not be forgotten, nor will the dream be denied that new generations will climb.

Through the kitchen window, looking to the east for the rising of the sun over Bunker Hill, the heart of lives is sometimes bright but just as often concealed in fog and cloud. The important thing is knowing it is there for the mulberry growing horizontally as well as vertically. The sparrows are grateful too, if gratitude is part of their plans or if "plan" is involved in the songs they sing. The mulberry aspires for breadth as well as height, which is a reminder to human beings, that stature is an individual matter. It's a reminder to the nearby tulip poplar, which we call "Judge," because it came from Gov. Bert T. Combs' Fern Hill in Powell County, a reminder that danger blows with its ill wind and now is the time to live.

The governor's widow, Sara, lives on as Chief Judge of the Kentucky Court of Appeals. She breathes the lovely air of Fern Hill, and she's generous with her trees and flowers from the hill reaching upward to the Powell County sky.

You see?

Here on Plum Lick, there's the young magnolia gracing the southern view from the breakfast table. Two lovers planted it there in loamy space dug with a common garden shovel, then watered and enriched it in the flowering of each new morning. One day, other lovers may kiss beneath the blossoms, and it won't matter who planted—only that joy lives.

Well, we've circled this old house as trees have embraced it on every side. The road leading in may one day be lined with sugar maples and dogwood, past the weeping willows and the sycamores taking root along the banks of Plum Lick Creek. We've saved the seed of the seasons, and yes, once there were these two people who decided the roadway to the home place should include trees carefully placed as keepsakes for the future. It would only be fitting that the two creations at the entrance would be the pair of purple plums, not as sentries questioning arrivals, or as honor guards in times of leaving, but as welcoming doormen as trusting as they are vigilant.

Trees are teachers and in the month of opening school doors, there's another opportunity for considering the lessons of the oak, the buckeye, and the locust.

That's why the old man mowing the tall grass in the verdant summer of 2004 decided to leave a volunteer locust sprig to grow and prosper on the eastern side of the house. The wish is that it become neither post nor firewood but as a sign of peace in this and every land.

Trees, like people, need room to breathe, becoming their truest selves without hurting others. Trees are reminders that Kentucky and all the world is a place for putting down lasting roots.

Tim

On July 4, 2005, Timothy Taylor was eighty-seven years upon the earth, the good earth, the comforter to be pulled up and patted upon our brows.

Tim's body has worn remarkably well (he has an artificial heart valve). He treats it with the same respect as he does the beloved grassland upon which he lives in the mantled forests of McCreary County. You can find him there in the midst of magnificent trees greening southeastern skies. For many years he has roamed with his wife, Peg, and their Border collie, Clyde, beneath the tulip poplar, oak, hemlock, sweet gum, dogwood, mountain magnolia, cedar, hickory, walnut, persimmon, and pine.

Humankind is blended with timber, where songbirds build their nests. To Timothy, a tree is not just a tree; it's a sustainable, renewal resource, each with its own purpose. Timothy has not been known for spending or the squandering of anything. Yet, he's not in favor of standing around doing nothing.

In one year alone, Timothy has planted one thousand trees.

He points to one of the true giants seeded long before his time, an American beech, probably four hundred years old. The notches on the towering behemoth mark the boundary where public land ends and private ownership begins. Some such trees, Timothy explains, have been known to make one thousand fine doors for houses.

Anybody who thinks the slim man with the shock of white hair has not been spry ought to try following Timothy Taylor through the Daniel Boone National Forest. On a Sunday afternoon, he wanted his visitors to experience a hidden waterfall on Rock Branch creek, another essential part of the ecology of man and his surroundings.

Along the way we savor the intricate delights of lady's slippers and discuss the possibilities of partridge peas.

Lifelong teachers, Timothy and Peg live nearby in a one hundred and thirty-three-year-old log cabin. Presently, she's the retired Director of the McCreary Center of Somerset Community College. He's retired from the University of Kentucky College of Agriculture but continues to consult.

We sit with Tim and Peg beneath a shady plum tree in the front yard at Good Spring Farm where, literally, weeds don't dare to grow. They don't favor the pain of sudden uprooting.

Most of his life, Timothy Taylor has been a scholar of grass and legumes—bluegrass, orchard grass, clover, alfalfa, tall fescue, and, of course, timothy. It is the grasslands working with the woodlands that provide life for human beings for thousands of years.

"We as practical people need to harvest trees. It is my practice to replant and nurture the forest," says Timothy.

Student and teacher at Cornell, Penn State, and the University of Kentucky, Dr. Taylor "retired" in 1985 to the place where he was born near Cumberland Falls.

A book cries out to be written about all this and, maybe, Timothy will get around to finishing his manuscript.

But, there's so much to do, and Timothy Taylor can't seem to resist doing it. There has been the kitchen garden to be kept just right, so that Peg need take only a few steps outside the back door to gather in lettuce, tomatoes, and prize asparagus. There have been the seven beef cows, the bull, and Peg's riding mare, Molly, to be rotated among five small pastures, each lush with grass that causes animals to know a good thing when they chew it.

Past his great-great-grandfather's millstone at the swinging garden gate, past the water barrel where the goldfish control the mosquitoes, past his father's sourwood walking stick leaning against the front door, inside this small cabin of hand-hewn tulip poplars are books in all directions.

In the sunroom where two pairs of binoculars are constantly available for bird watching, there's a mini-arsenal of books: *Kentucky Birds, The Audubon Society Field Guide to North American Birds, Eastern Region, Weeds of Kentucky and Adjacent States, The Audubon Society Field Guide to North American Insects & Spiders, Trees & Shrubs of Kentucky,* and *Peterson's Field Guide, Eastern Birds.*

Timothy Taylor's byword, which could be a password for many who care about heritage and the future: "I try to do the things that I judge to be important."

Timothy's words can be interpreted many ways. The challenge in understanding his fundamental values lives in simple, grassroots reality.

Whittlers of Cedar

A knife has a life of its own. Especially when sharpened just right for whittling.

We'll not forget the whittlers of cedar on the front porch of Blevin's Grocery in Preston, east of Stepstone, north of Hope, a short way from Peeled Oak in Bath County.

We wrote about whittlers ten years ago in *The Quiet Kentuckians*. In January of 2005, David picked up the phone and spoke howdy over there to Blevin's Grocery alongside the old Chesapeake and Ohio track.

It was good to know that Roscoe Cassidy had turned ninety-six years old.

Postmistress Helen Blevins called Roscoe to the phone, and we asked about his health.

"Pretty good."

"How do you stay healthy?"

"Lord, I don't know—good pasture and water."

"Still whittling?"

"Not when the weather's bad. When warm weather comes I sit on the front porch and whittle."

"What's your favorite knife?"

"Like 'em all. Sit around and trade knives. Voss Cut's the best."

There are so many knives these days—Owl Head's another favorite. So are Puma and Hen and Rooster.

We didn't talk long about all the knife possibilities, because quiet Kentuckians are not known for gabbing. Better to get on with the blade on the edge of the business.

"When March rolls around, we'll come visit," we offered.

"Come over and we'll whittle awhile," Roscoe concluded.

We'll miss whittlers Oscar Copher and Roy "Johnny" Donahue, who've passed on, but Coon Conyers may still be of amind to build a morning of shavings, and we'll be on the lookout for him. And Sam Ingram, he'll pull up a chair and open his good knife—we whittlers have got a right smart whittling to do before the big sundown.

Ten years ago, when I returned from Preston to Plum Lick, I asked Rube Blevins if I could bring some shavings back home.

"We'll sack you up some of it," said Rube, who'd already treated me to a baloney sandwich.

When I arrived home, I asked my wife to close her eyes: "Now smell."

She like to not stop crying.

Said it reminded her of her father.

He used to be a whittler of cedar.

Springtime

It's a comfort being on the edge of spring in Kentucky—time of yellow bells, traces of snow, winds tingling windowpanes.

It's the promising side of one of the four inter-seasons, when weather vagaries lead to bad raps—weather's the damnedest in Kentucky: find the snow shovel, track through the house, muddy the rugs; slush today, flash flood tomorrow; drivers don't know how to drive or row their boats. You've heard the gibes.

So, what do the furriners, the outlanders want? Winter in Buffalo? Summer in Key West? Hurricane season along the Gulf Coast? It could be arranged.

Each one of those predictable places has a private spot in native hearts, yet there's a loyal bunch of us in Kentucky who value other precious certainties—mourning doves *who-whooing* before and after showers, defying forecasts. Mist and fog splay up the valley from Plum—long-legged lightning cracks, thunder crashes—cover of snow skiffed to the chin of the new garden out back.

Three more weeks of "winter?"

There ought to be a better name for it.

Maybe "Win-spring." This helps to identify the idea of earning spring, which means there's precious time to plan for a better garden. May we also say that garden is another word for life?

How're the tomato seedlings coming along? Are they soaking up the sun coming through the kitchen window? And the yellow bells. Have they awakened any springtime notions in a wintry noggin? (We call them yellow bells, you may prefer jonquils. Or daffodils.)

What's in a name? Not as much as we too often think. It's the idea that counts—the rich, loamy feeling of possibilities, the excitement of change.

"March Madness" doesn't have to mean slam dunks.

It can mean the awakening time of the year.

It can mean rebirth.

Maybe, the spring of 2005 is the year of revisiting grandparents, asking them the seediest of questions. How did you grow your vineyard, your garden? What were your favorite flowers? Your favorite vegetables? Teach me some tricks of the soil so that I can pass them along to my children and their children.

And we'll tell you what we'll do! We'll bring you fresh flowers and vegetables from our garden, and we'll re-decorate your window-sill. There might even be room for a window box! And when things are growing outside this summer, we'll come and fetch you and show you what we've managed to do together. We'll sit beneath the water maples and speak of times gone by and good times yet to come.

We'll speak of hope.

We'll resist the temptation to say that our vineyard, our strawberry patch, our beans and potatoes are better than our neighbor's.

We'll say a little prayer for peace.

We'll remember to share the wealth that springs from our garden.

Have we strayed? Hunkered down? Surely not.

For every car bomb, each scene of

violence on television, every spoken word of anger in the cold corridors of winters past, every envious thought upon our lying down and our arising for another gifted day, let's sow one more positive seed for spring.

We flow through Kentucky springs with some days wetter than others, some days more dew-draped than others, here a pleasant breeze, there an aggravating snow spate. But it is what it is and there's nothing to do about it but get up and move if the problem becomes too much trouble to resolve.

It's Kentucky, a state of mind, and we here on Plum Lick cast our vote in favor of it.

The hosta lilies from Pleasant Valley plantation and the magnolia transplant from Mississippi are making their annual resurgence, and for that we say, "Thank y'all." We know you'd rather be down there in the land of the live oak and the Spanish moss, but we do appreciate your generous accommodation to our need for you to be here with us. We'd be happy to send to your friends a little planting or two from up here. One thing for sure: we don't want your fire ants. So, you can keep them there and figure out what to do with them.

Our water maples—the old timers and the new sprigs—are celebrating the arrival of another Kentucky summer and to give thanks for it we get down on our popping knees and sing a hallelujah chorus.

If the June bugs want to join in they'll do it at their own peril. We put them in the same general category as the seventeen-year cicada, those voracious critters born hungry to die hungry in a noisy, crackling brown condition.

It's the year of the seventeen-year cicada, and it could be considerably off-putting if not down right wretched to contemplate. However, we have it on good authority that whatever buggy thing happens in the summer of 2004, it definitely could be a whole lot worse.

The Department of Entomology (study of insects, a.k.a. bugs) at the University of Kentucky has sent out good news.

According to entomologist Lee Townsend: "Cicadas neither bite nor sting so they pose no threat to people or animals. They may be attracted to vibrations from equipment—mowers, weed eaters, and such, but are not swarming to attack the operator. This may not appear to be the case to the operator at the time, however. Cicada generally will try to escape if approached and males will emit a loud alarm buzz if handled but that is the best that they can do. Males are responsible for the 'din' associated with cicadas as they join sound in a chorus of calling songs that attract both males and females on high sunlit branches of trees."

We spoke on the last day of March with Professor Townsend to get a better understanding about where we Kentuckians and the seventeen-year cicada will be by June, and he said a lot of the action will have wound down by late April. Some activity would still be going on in May over much of the commonwealth, but northern Kentucky would still be having some problems in June, especially along the edges of wooded areas.

The female cicada likes to lay her eggs in bark split by "blade-like ovipositors." Young trees could become deformed by it, but in the main it's a case of "noisy curiosity."

"Twigs weakened by egg-laying slits will break, causing 'flagging' or browning of the tips of the branches. Pruning may be needed to compensate for damage to branch architecture on small landscape trees."

You might want to check with your county agent concerning control—to decide whether to cover, spray, or prune.

We've given the matter a certain amount of thought, but not too much. All though it may hurt their feelings, we've decided to go on with our hallelujah chorus and let the seventeen-year cicada go hang.

"Hold April!"

Despite the shuttle disaster in early 2003, when seven of the best and brightest were scattered like stardust over the Texas sky, there comes this special time of the year in which to restore innocence and uphold the promise of creation.

"Hold April" were the words of the Kentucky poet Jesse Stuart, who spoke with fervent hope embraced in beholding the glory of rebirth from frozen depths of winter to flowerings of another spring.

Fragile human beings are powerless to hold back termination and resurrection, Jesse taught with passion, his words borne from his W-Hollow heritage in Greenup County. Born in a tiny mountain shack, his birth and youth predated modern highways and consolidated schools, long before astronauts walked on the moon and moved ever closer to rendezvous with Mars.

Hold April! A collection of Jesse's heart-driven writings reaches out through time and space to cradle eternity, yearning to orbit beyond mortal defeat to immortal triumph.

> *After I spoke to Death and shook his hand*
> *He left me with my new lease on life.*
> *I vowed the second half should not be spent in vain.*

Jesse wrote for the common man, woman, and child and would hardly be at home with cynicism such as Eliot's "stirring dull roots with spring rain." Jesse, the rough-hewn Kentuckian, would find more blessed satisfaction out there on Bridges's "blossoming boughs of April."

Jesse would be full of life or he'd be none.

His people have known the twists and turns of Little Sandy with headwaters arising in Elliott, tumbling through Sandy Hook northeast through Carter and Greenup Counties.

From out this land, these "dark hills" mirrored with the promise of flowering dogwood, Jesse Stuart emerged. After college he returned home to W-Hollow to become and write *Man with a Bull-Tongue Plow* and weaver of *The Thread That Runs So True*.

Hold April!

Those of us who've come to a better understanding of Jesse and ourselves (the intellectuals at Vanderbilt did not quite welcome him as a prodigal son) now see that the bloodroot of Kentucky Earth lives on through education—not by rote but by gentle reasoning, not by packaged videotex but by one-on-one teacher-to-student and parent relationships. What a challenge on this journey through Space!

Whenever we revisit Jesse Hilton Stuart (1906-1984)—we're reminded of the need to be one's self, first and foremost. We don't wish to be cloned. We wish to be true to ourselves, and we should want those who follow to stand on shoulders inherited from pioneers who've passed down this valley on the way through the cosmos.

Jesse made this notion as clear and pure as highland spring water:

> *I sing of mountain men, their lives and loves*
> *And mountain waters and the wild-bird cries...*

Stuart's ancestors and ours fought in the American Revolution, on dark and bloody ground before Kentucky was a state. In the next century, Kentuckians were furiously on both sides of the Civil War. Then came the feuds, and other barriers to peaceful accord on

31

common ground in nature with perpetual relationship to soil and water.

April is more than troubled weather forecasting. It's the month of possibilities, stepping forward to meet the new day for pioneers of body, mind, and spirit.

Kentuckians understand the coming of another April, and they have welcomed it. Never mind spring freshets and flash floods, we've been well-rooted and watered in the countryside.

In 2003, the view from W-Hollow to Plum Lick was written in February blue of Texas sky. And now, each one of us—whether we be astronaut or standing earthbound at home—each in our own intuitive way, have a foretaste of glory.

As Jesse might have said, hold April in the cupped hands of a new beginning, and splash it on the face of despair. Know it and love it for what it is—this turbulent passage through eons designed and ruled by the creator of the universe.

Flow

If you take a look at Lalie's drawing of a "map" of Kentucky, you'll see that there are no interstate highways, no toll roads or parkways, no county or state lines, and no towns.

There are only the rivers of the state.

When you look at the map you know what it is—Kentucky!

Lalie came up with this original idea after she thought about how best to illustrate our *Rivers of Kentucky*.

She wanted something simple and powerful, something that showed how our rivers define Kentuckians. Sure, interstate highways are essential and towns represent markets for our products, but without the state's water system we'd be dry bones.

The theory that "all the water that's here now was here in the beginning, and all the water that's here now is all the water there'll ever be," is an idea we took with us to "Shaped by Water #2, A Conference for Women of Eastern Kentucky." It was held April 6, 2002, at Leslie County Cooperative Extension Service in Hyden, just off Route 80 between Manchester and Hazard on the middle fork of the Kentucky River.

The sponsors were The Center for Appalachian Studies at Eastern Kentucky University and the Kentucky Foundation for Women.

Objectives included "Recognition of rural women as leaders and guardians of their community watersheds."

The goals of the conference included: "...to help others identify projects they would like to do which will help promote awareness of the environmental, economic, historic and cultural importance of eastern Kentucky's waterways through the arts." We like the notion of combining art, humanity, and the movement of water, because it binds all of us together as a better community.

The conference leaders said, "All you need to bring are ideas, and an open mind."

Well, we hoped our mind hadn't slammed shut on us, at least not yet, and as for an idea to share with others: we'd like to continue writing about Kentucky's waterways whenever we have the opportunity. Of course, writing and talking are one thing—doing is the frosting on the cake.

When we spoke with Judy Sizemore, one of the conference co-directors, she said "Shaped by Water basically started out as a woman's project, but we don't leave the men out. It's a good starting point, connecting with your waterways, and not just water, connecting to heritage and culture as a whole."

Judy is a writer working with the Kentucky Arts Council. Co-director Pat Banks is a visual artist, who lives on the Kentucky River and paints Kentucky riverscapes. Gabrielle Beasley, the third co-director, is a photographer and videographer.

None of us expects overnight miracles, and we recognize that cleaning up our rivers, creeks, licks, and branches is going to last beyond our lifetime. But the dream is to pass along an awareness of the importance of water and its relationship to human beings.

It begins at home.

Doesn't do much good to gripe about polluted waters in somebody else's neighborhood if we don't take care of water on the land where we live. The last thing we ever want to do is to dump anything in somebody else's stream, not a chewing gum wrapper or oil change from our riding mower. Washing machines and dryers don't belong in anybody's creek or river.

In the Upper Gorge of Red River, up there in Wolfe County in the Hazel Green area, Russ Miller has led a ten-year campaign to clean up the stream strewn with car and truck tires, refrigerators, and television sets. Russ Miller and other volunteers have marked and raised the heinous litter and floated it down to collection points.

Eight miles of boulders pointing skyward on a dangerous stretch of stream—"Dog Drowning Hole" and "Canoe Eating Rock"—the Upper Gorge of Kentucky's Red River deserves respect and stewardship. Every year, an estimated two hundred tires are dumped into the water, which should be and can be pristine again.

There are other more complex water pollution issues that must be addressed legislatively, but we wish that were not so. Who knows, maybe if we Kentuckians spread the word through artistic talent that pollution of streams is wrong, the idea of committed water stewardship will grow. Unless individuals accept responsibility for a cooperative effort, we may find some of our streams so polluted we'll be able to walk across them without getting our feet wet.

There's no reason why our Kentucky culture can't be known for the most unpolluted water in the United States. But, that won't happen until we understand that a natural waterway is not a sewer pipe or a junkyard.

So, it comes down to this: what else can we know about the water falling from the sky and onto our roof? What else can we learn about the water in the ground and moving on toward its destiny? How can we help educate our selves and others about the value of clean water?

Millstones

The book of Revelations compares the punishment of Babylon to a mighty angel heaving a huge millstone into the sea.

A "millstone around the neck" is a stern reminder of certain destruction after a lifetime of trudging along the path of unforgiving travail.

Yet, Shelley's "mill-wheel sound" savors the comforting notion of permanence and stability.

Here on Plum Lick, Missus and I only wish we had a millstone or two to brag about—something to greet the yuppies of our time. Instead, we turn for guidance to the Kentucky Old Mill Association for a renewal of faith that all unselfish efforts amount to something and will one day be rewarded.

At the turn of the new century, six "old mill nuts"—Fred Coy Jr., Harry Enoch, Dennis Feeback, Tom Fuller, Larry Meadows and Eugene Peck—held a meeting at the Red River Museum in Clay City, where there are about forty millstones, twenty-four grindstones and twenty grist mills.

"SPOOM," the Society for the Preservation of Old Mills, was off to the races, where water and gravity have their way, and the organization's newsletter—*The Millstone*—has quickly become a who's who of millstone memorabilia with a yarn or two thrown in for good measure.

For instance, the Volume Four, Number One issue for 2005 includes stories about Wolf Pen Branch Mill, Pine Hill Valley Mill, Early Mills of Bourbon County, and Mills from Dawn Comes to the Mountains. Kentucky place names suggest a theme of continuity—a state of mind remembering the past, thriving in the present, and longing for the future.

It goes without saying, millstones aren't known to be found on grocery shelves along with a parade of competing quick mixes— instant biscuit and cornbread lovers armed with zipped-up plastic bags need not apply.

Miracles of grooved rock respond only to a combination of moving water, gravity and a flood of human ingenuity—a reminder of how far we've dipped into the modern world of sliced bread and glazed doughnuts.

Fred E. Coy, Jr. has written about Frank Perry, who "had a wealth of knowledge about the many varied goings-on in the upper reaches of Red River.

"Mr. Perry explained that his father would take a big flat rock and made grooves in it that extended over the edge. Then he would gather rich pine from an old stump and split it into small pieces. The pieces were stood on their ends in the middle of the rock and set on fire. As soon as it was burning well, he would place an upside-down kettle over the pine slowly burned, the pine tar would run down the grooves in the rock and into a container. When we asked about the use of pine tar, Mr. Perry said that the gristmills in those days had no metal bearings, they were made entirely of wood and pine tar was used for lubrication."

Here's the thing—

One day, we just might have to pull back from the mad rush of instant gratification. We might be called upon to start over again after sputtering out on the high-tech, looping yellow brick road. Engines may run dry of energy and computers may be hacked to death.

Oil may go undiscovered.

Armageddon may come sooner than we dare imagine.

If there's one last chance for a sturdy few to sit down quietly by a millstone, it might be a good, positive idea to know how it was in the beginning.

In her classic *Seedtime On the Cumberland*, Harriette Arnow traces the evolution of the eighteenth-century, water-powered mill... "as a rule there were mill days, once or twice a week, or in dry weather the miller with a small pond might have to stop grinding for weeks together, and when mill day at last came it was in the nature of a community reunion."

"United We Stand, Divided We Fall" is the long-suffering motto for the Commonwealth of Kentucky, which has survived the Civil War, family feuds, and ongoing political divisions.

It might be a good idea to gather 'round the old millstone and offer the firm handshake of trust, which foresees rich, new, intrastate possibilities.

Drought

A west Kentucky farmer—face creased, eyes moist, soft whistle riding on his dusty breath—once said: "Hardly ever rains durin' a drought."

A geologist proclaimed: "All the water that's here now was here in the beginning, and all the water that's here now is all the water there'll ever be."

Booker T. Washington said: "Put your bucket down where you are."

"But I can't put my bucket down in the subdivision where I live, the ground is caked and cracked. Can't put my bucket down in the high-rise condominium where I reside, for me there is no ground," you cry.

Put your bucket down inside yourself and consider a community's need that conservation of water is a year-round passion, drought or no drought.

Urban and rural survivors of the worst drought in Kentucky in many memories can put their collective buckets down. They can vote their support for improved water development projects.

The water is there and it will always be there, but it may not be available exactly in the time frame or the quality that human beings have a right to expect it.

The great hydrologic circling begins with the outcropping of springs feeding headwaters of licks, branches, creeks, and rivers rolling to the sea. The surface water is only a mirror of the hidden aquifers, where ground water percolates.

Human beings don't live on or alongside these patterns of water, they are an essential part of it. Adult body weight is about fifty-five to seventy percent (baby body weight is as much as eighty percent). We can get along without food a lot longer than we can without water, therefore it's a serious irony that so many Americans take water, expecially drinking water, for granted.

There's a reminder in the *Complete Home Medical Guide:* "The body is often likened to a self-contained sea in which every body cell is constantly bathed in salty water."

A drought is a doctor's wake-up call, but the insensitive, bad-habit side of us dulls awareness of the life-or-death realities of water.

The drought of '99 has reaffirmed the good fortune of having deep wells here on Plum Lick where we live and where we hope to die of some cause other than thirst.

But, wells alone are not enough. Ground water needs protection from surface pollutants. Chemicals and animal wastes can contaminate the purity of water, a problem to be solved.

Kentucky water flows to the Ohio, to the Mississippi, and to the Gulf of Mexico, where we are blessed with the miracle of evaporation. The sun draws the water up into the clouds, winds return the clouds to Kentucky, the rains fall, and the cycle is completed.

It is a natural phenomenon that competes with a habit of misuse. In his book *Nor Any Drop to Drink*, William Ashworth has written: "... breathing filtered air whose temperature has been determined by the flick of a dial, we can be forgiven for assuming that what the natural world does is no longer of concern to us." And yet, when we are alone on a desert island, forgiveness matters little to dusty throats.

The drought of '99 has been more than an inconvenience, a

vexation that annoys. It is a reality and a stern reminder that the water movement, what Ashworth calls "the great planetary water engine that drives all life on this green and rolling earth," should never be taken for granted.

"It's kind of drizzling outside," my wife says to me on an early autumn morning. That is the good news. Let us go forth today resolved to be a better steward of what the Great Creator has provided, Challenge us to remember to know the value of water, protect and conserve it to the best of our ability, and pass along this knowledge to those generations still to be born in this sea called life.

Kentucky Bend

Kentucky Bend is space, silence, and sloughs.

Some call it Madrid Bend.

Tennesseeans call it Bessie's Bend.

In March, farmers in the Bend will be getting ready to plant corn and fertilize wheat. A constant worry is blowing wind bowling stems over, making the harvest less bountiful. Families know this to be true, but they don't allow themselves the luxury of fretting aloud. They are tough because they know all farmers must be tough.

Adrienne Stepp walks to the front door with confidence born and bred by the river. She needs only to be told that Kenneth said a visit would be in order, for when Kenneth Lynn says something, she'll bank on it. An eighty-six-year old matriarch has her fond reminiscences, her earned privileges, but she needs a sidekick with a strong arm, a straight back, and an honest disposition.

That spells, Kenneth.

"Come in," says Adrienne, taking the center place on a comfortable couch.

"I've lived on the Mississippi all my life," says Adrienne, widow of Alfred, who once vowed he'd spend every penny he had to keep the State of Tennessee from petitioning the Bend away from Kentucky.

In the beginning, there were four thousand acres, but over the years Alfred and Adrienne saw the acreage reduced by necessity born of capricious, mainly declining, then, vanishing markets. Four silos stand empty—the cattle operation has ceased because it wasn't making a profit. The hogs are gone—they weren't paying their way. There's no livestock in the Kentucky Bend—only corn, wheat, and soybeans.

Adrienne speaks in an even tone muted by a go-round last year with pneumonia and a recurring bronchial condition. She calls out, friendly like, to the other room: "Barbara and Lucy, you all come on in here."

Two younger steel magnolias appear—Barbara, wife of Kenneth, and "Lucy" (Mary Catherine), their daughter. Sentinels, they've been invited into Captain's quarters to relax from housekeeping jobs. They take places, protectively, on either side of Adrienne. They are long-suffering as the conversation returns to water.

"Wished the flood wouldn't get us about every year," says Mary Catherine, perpetual apprehension checked for the moment.

Mary Catherine Reynolds, twenty-seven years old, wife of Michael, mother of two sons, Hunter and Joshua, sits resolutely on one end of the couch on the downstream side.

Mary Catherine's mother, Barbara Lynn, sits on the other end of the couch beneath the window overlooking Watson Lake, usually a pleasant finger of water.

In the center of the couch, the benefactress, Adrienne, owns more than two thousand acres of the total fifteen thousand acres in the Kentucky Bend. Proud of her life's work, she wouldn't want to be anyplace else. Alfred had come there in the late '20s, and he and Adrienne were married in 1954. Of Adrienne's approximately one thousand cultivated acres, four hundred are in corn, one hundred in wheat, and six hundred are in beans, more or less. Knowing when to plant, when to fertilize, when to harvest are things not learned readily from books. It takes a personal, watchful eye on the levee, the river, and the sky.

43

"Straight rows — Kenneth doesn't like crooked rows," says Adrienne with a mellifluous southern accent.

"Don't care about TV, rather read," she says, looking forward to the regular arrival of the bookmobile from Hickman. She confesses that she does turn on television when the Mississippi begins to rise and another flood is headed around the bend. "I go by the river gauge at New Madrid. When the water comes and begins to cross the road, I watch television from Paducah and Cape Girardeau."

Sometimes Adrienne puts aside fiction and holds a meeting of the Kentucky Bend Levee Board. She is vice-president and Barbara Lynn is secretary treasurer. "We mow the levee, grade it, pick up chunks after high water," says Adrienne.

"What kind of trees are here?"

"Cypress, cottonwood, pecan — sixty-six-acre pecan woods," says Adrienne.

"What do you do for entertainment?"

"We stay home, don't give anybody any trouble. We play a lot of cards," says the matriarch with a sense of calm contentment.

"The church bus was a form of entertainment," says Mary Catherine.

"Bicycles. Wheelers."

"Wheelers?"

"Four-wheelers," says Barbara.

"Garden, farm, and fish. Sometimes too quiet," says Mary Catherine, like a doe with some impatience, weary with the cares of survival.

"What do you fish?

"Crappie, catfish, some bass," says Adrienne. "Those little round fish give a fight. When I was a young girl, we'd go to Cairo and meet the Engineers' Boat. We'd ride down around the Kentucky Bend, get off at Tiptonville, and have dinner at Reelfoot."

"And today — peace and quiet?"

"Yes, and I'm thankful to the Good Lord," says the sturdy little lady.

Kenneth Lynn died March 23, 2001. He's buried with his father in Antioch Cemetery in Hornbeak, Tennessee.

Adrienne Stepp passed away two years ago. She's at peace beside her husband in the Pickway Cemetery at Hickman.

The house stands vacant.

Everything inside is just as it was when we first visited. Nearby, Barbara Lynn, her son, Donald, and his wife have made a fresh start with a "beautiful crop of beans."

And now there's a granddaughter.

Her name is Adrianna.

She's three years old.

Building Dams

With April showers upon us, it might be high time to build a dam and back up some future water here on the farm. This doesn't mean just another piddling sky pond or a bigger bedroom for croaking frogs. It means something that stands a good chance of making a big difference—something that goes beyond our selfish selves. Call it a nice gift to neighbors and generations to come.

The heart of the matter is responsibility for better control of the flow of surface water on the piece of land where we live. Deep down in the ground there's an overflowing natural resource for use rather than abuse. Too often, it's ignored altogether.

In the best of times, when conservation is abandoned, topsoil is gradually swept away. The destruction usually only makes headlines in flood years.

There's a road map for it.

The water "begins" in eastern Kentucky, but its destination, its destiny is toward the southwest—through the Ohio and the Mississippi channels—and the movement of soil and water is monumental.

It's past the point of building up the Mississippi Delta. That's our precious earth down there. It's one thing to be taxed on it, it's another thing to give it away after we've paid the sheriff.

They've got so much Kentucky soil at the mouth of the Mississippi River it's beginning to choke the life out of the Louisiana ecology.

Where do we fit into this mess?

Here in Kentucky, we don't have Minnesota's ten thousand lakes, but we do have a unique system of more than sixty reservoirs, some huge, many exceedingly small, from another promising sunrise over Crank's Creek Lake in Harlan County to another forgiving sunset beyond Watson Lake in Fulton.

Fishing is supreme, a paradise, in Cumberland, Barkley, and Kentucky Lakes.

In all directions, there are countless opportunities for soil and water stewardship. At the same time, there's an outstanding variety of recreational choices, a chance to get away and each time experience a different locale.

After we camp, canoe, fish, hike, hunt, or simply view wildlife, we may want to bring back a fundamental idea to the place where we permanently park our horses, hang our hats, and prop up our feet.

Water conservation makes good common sense. Rather than complain about the vagaries of the Kentucky water dilemma, time might be better spent cooperating with Mother Nature.

It could be as simple as turning off the condominium faucet while we brush our urban teeth. There's a piper to pay each time a lawn or garden is watered from a hose. Near rural communities, it could mean calling in the bulldozers and developing more strategically located impoundments as a way to minimize flash floods and maximize water availability during droughts.

The moisture returns in April and throughout the year, but the soil does not come back. That's a reality that ought to make us think more carefully when we waste water by not fixing the smallest dripping faucet. Each handful of dirt ought to be a serious consideration. Every excavation should be planned around a central idea: how does this affect other people?

There'll be tradeoffs, and they should not be forgotten or taken lightly. For every Land Between the Lakes there's a Land Between the Rivers. Huge impoundments involve huge relocations of human beings, and every effort should be made to be as fair as we are farseeing. It takes inspired, unselfish individuals to address the common good.

Here on the runnels of Plum Lick—rills, rivulets, and springs—we'll not be displacing homesteads. We may be stirring and restructuring memories, but we

can't live in the past. The present and the future are calling with strong voices. They're saying, we should have a vision.

How fine it will be to be known as the state that cares the most for what it has: plenty of water, priceless land, and good-hearted people who understand what's at stake.

River of Ages

Cissels River isn't long enough to be a river, some might say. Many believe a stream has to be a hundred miles long before it can be a "river."

Well, if you want to know the plain truth about it, rivers are rivers because somebody has the cheek to call them rivers.

Such a man came up to us at Ham Days in Lebanon in Marion County, took one look at our book *Rivers of Kentucky* and asked, "Cissels River in there?"

He had us.

As soon as we found two minutes to rub together, we left Plum Lick Creek and went down to the headwaters of Cissels River. West out of Lebanon, we spotted the beginning of the little stream close by Toad Mattingly Road.

Cissels River flows over large, flat rocks until it empties into Hardin's Creek, where a large box elder guards the confluence. Cissels River is three miles by road, longer by twists and turns.

Cissel or Cissell is another way of spelling Cecil. We found Charles M. ("Mike") Cecil on the edge of the St. Mary community, and he explained that his great-great-great grandfather Matthew Cissell settled here in 1785. His son became a "Cecil" and that's the name that lives on through Mike's four children and ten grandchildren.

The grandfather clock in the corner of the home place has only stopped twice—once when Mike's wife died, the other time when Mike had a heart attack.

"There was no one to wind the clock."

As for Cissels River:

"All I knew it by when I was growing up was Cissels River. I fished in it—blue gill, sun perch, catfish. Deepest holes four to six feet. Runs most of the year, real dry summer, it'll dry up. Few snakes in it. Hunted ground hog," says Mike. "Groundhog is like mutton, longer you chew groundhog the bigger it gets. 'Cissels River Pike' is now Loretto Highway," he goes on.

Hardin's Creek forms the Marion-Washington County line. After flowing past Maker's Mark Distillery, Hardin's empties into Beech Fork at the Nelson County line, part of the area sometimes called America's Holy Land.

Mike Cecil is the cantor at St. Charles Church, second oldest Catholic Church west of the Alleghenies. Father Charles Nerinckx, who fled from religious persecution in St. Mary's County, Maryland, founded St. Charles Church, in 1786.

Holy Cross in Marion County is the oldest Catholic Church on the Kentucky frontier.

Mike took us through another house on the farm, the one built by his great-grandfather, in 1879, after he returned from the Civil War and found everything burned to the ground. We walked into the hallway where Mike's grandfather long ago lay in state, stood in the room where Mike's father was born and died, the room where Mike was born fifty-five years ago. There were the family washstand and the steamer trunk.

He showed us the gnarled pear tree as old as the 1789 house, and we walked by the cistern, the grindstone, and the 1785 Concord grape vines that came from Maryland. Mike dug up a clump of cannas, his favorite flower, for us to take home along with a coffee tree bean for planting next spring.

"I got my love of plants from my mother, Nina Mae," Mike said, pointing to the ginkgo tree, the Chinese chestnut, the ornamental purple butter beans, mock orange, Roma and the mountain yellow tomatoes, the Mississippi ivy, the Kansas sunflowers, Florida poinsettia, Maryland lilac, and the thirteen varieties of tame Kentucky blackberries.

We sat awhile to look at family pictures, and we read from the old St. Mary's College yearbook:

"We are truly heirs of all the ages: and as honest men it behooves us to learn the extent of our inheritance."

On our quiet way home near year's end, we passed through the little Cisselville crossroads, and the last thing in blessed sight was the American flag flying high from a slender pole attached to the highway sign.

Three Hundred Springs

It's a place like no other—hallowed ground, where Indians long ago camped...cool and refreshing, where witch hazel seeds itself... mushrooms hover as big as a man's hat...old oaks, red elms, horse chestnuts, and sycamores tower...and rare maidenhair fern grows without parallel in the world.

It's called Three Hundred Springs.

You might say, it's a quiet, Cupid kind of place, detached from the run and go, the kiss and tell of the superhighway, I-65, in Hart County, Kentucky.

Geologist and historian Dr. Willard Rouse Jillson (1890-1975) described this water wonder as "bridal veil-falls," which is apt today, because on the high bluff above the outpouring, ninety-three-year-old W.O. (William Oscar) Buckner lives with his eighty-nine-year-old valentine Marie Dangerfield Buckner.

They've been married seventy years.

She has a pacemaker now, and he's proud of his artificial knees. "I told the doctor he made only one little mistake," says W.O. "He said, 'What's that?' I said, 'You didn't leave a scar for me to brag about,'" laughs Mr. Buckner as he leads us down the slippery-sloping, old mill road for a better look at Three Hundred Springs.

Marie stays in the century-old house to mind one of her jam cakes and awaits the return of the hikers. "Can't do nothing with him," she's been heard to fret.

Sheba, the four-year-old Australian shepherd goes in front. Just the other day, she distracted a bull that wanted to have W.O. for lunch.

"I squalled and waved my arms. Sheba worked on him from the other end," says Mr. Buckner going down the leaf-, limb-, and rock-strewn slope as if his knees belonged to a nineteen-year-old.

"Your wife said to watch out for copperhead snakes," we say, trying to keep up.

"No copperheads out this time of the year," says W.O.

"Saw a bobcat the other day."

"What did he look like?"

"Brownish color. Didn't stop for me to look at him. He looked taller, because he was more in the air than he was on the ground." W.O. winks, "I'm careful where I walk."

Suddenly, there's the Mother Spring of Three Hundred Springs! Water gushing out as clear and cold as the instant it was born "over yonder on Maxie's Knob." From a cliff overhang looking like a natural grotto, sparkling water cascades on a sharp forty-five degree angle to form an eighty-five-foot waterfall straight down into Green River.

Sight to behold!

Springtime is the best time to experience Three Hundred Springs, when the water "roars," says Ray Jewell, who farms in Round Bottom on the other side of the river. During the wet seasons, water springs from the earth in uncommon numbers, hence the name Three Hundred Springs. The best way to view the glorious spectacle of the falling water and the maidenhair fern is from a canoe or a broad-bottomed boat.

Standing beneath the waterfall is not advised. Not good for fern or fellow. As W.O. describes the feeling: "Strip off, hump up, and get out—you can't stay."

We walk to the site of a nineteenth century water-powered gristmill. All that's left are a pair of millstones, part of the foundation, and memories of Marie's grandfather, Milam, who worked there. She has a treasured picture of him and his bride.

Their descendants, W.O. and Marie, are living today, she smiles, "Just like country people—do as we please."

Marie has slices of jam cake waiting on small dishes and freshly made coffee poured when we return and are powerfully needful of a pick-us-up.

"I can't write books but I can bake cakes and I want you to have it," says Marie.

W.O. has stopped to gather a bucket of turnips for us to take home along with a piece of driftwood, a water table rock, and a piece from W.O.'s collection of rock with a petrified snail from the time when Three Hundred Springs was, we guess, part of a great prehistoric sea.

In 2005, Marie Buckner was still making jam pies and W.O. had another new knee. Marie was right there in the Nashville hospital room before and after the procedure. Three Tennessee Titan football players heard about the man in his nineties getting a new knee and they came in to visit. They wanted to know what was W.O.'s game plan. And they might have left feeling better about each time they "took a knee" to win a game.

Marie told them it was simple. She'd been taking care of him for seventy years. Even back when W.O. and Marie celebrated their fiftieth anniversary, somebody wanted to know what was the secret to married bliss.

Again, Marie said, it was simple, "We got married—there was nothing out there any better."

Hell fer Sartin

Hell fer Sartin is in Leslie County.

Some write it Hell for Certain, because there's an understandable disagreement over which is the more correct way. Those who prefer "Hell for Certain" tend to believe "Hell fer Sartin" is another Appalachian put off on. Actually, it's a celebration of strong-as-an-ox individuals and down-home values with a generous dollop of common sense.

The late Leonard W. Roberts wrote a book titled *South from Hell-fer-Sartin*, and Kentucky author John Fox Jr. had a royal field day writing in dialect. *His Little Shepherd of Kingdom Come* and *The Trail of the Lonesome Pine* favor Hell fer Sartin fer sure.

The little rocky stream—Hell fer Sartin—arises in northwestern Leslie County, near Sizemore, where Bull Skin Creek slides westward to the south fork of the Kentucky River at Oneida, in Clay County. Hell fer Sartin tumbles eastward to the middle fork of the Kentucky. Between Sizemore and the mouth of Hell fer Sartin at Confluence, there's only one place name on today's map and that's Kaliope, pronounced KAL-ee-OH-pee, which is somehow connected with a man who ran a Greek restaurant in Hazard, and he came over to marry a young lady from Hell fer Sartin.

Cutshin Creek is also in Leslie County to the east of the county seat, Hyden, and there's a place on the map named Cutshin. According to *The Kentucky Encyclopedia*, the names "Cutshin" and "Hell fer Sartin" (the *Encyclopedia* chooses to spell it that way) came about as the result of an early pioneer, who tried to cross the streams during stormy weather. It was hell fer sartin and he cut his shin. Something like that.

You might want to read Robert M. Rennick's *From Red Hot to Monkey's Eyebrow*, which sheds more light on this subject of unusual Kentucky place names. And, of course, there's Dr. Niel Plummer's *Guide To The Pronunciation of Kentucky Towns and Cities*. For example, Yosemite is pronounced YOH-se-mite.

Leonard W. Roberts also compiled *Up Cutshin & Down Greasy: Folkways of a Kentucky Mountain Family*, which was published by the University Press of Kentucky. Greasy Creek is in Harlan County, and "Greasy" doesn't mean what a outlander might think. It just means a little slippery after a nice rain.

Cutshin, a longer stream than Hell fer Sartin, arises near Big Rock close to the Harlan County line. Cutshin flows northward through Yeaddiss, Smilax, and on to Wooten, where the waters merge with Meetinghouse and Flackley branches. We need help on how these names came to be.

As good fate would have it, our path crossed with Eliza, daughter of William Curtis Wooten, who made a living rafting logs, trading horses, and raising cattle. Eliza, born on Cutshin, in 1918, taught first, second, and third grades at Hell fer Sartin school. Back in the thirties, Eliza and another teacher hung a curtain to make a two-room school out of a one-room school.

We had a grand time talking about the old days, before there were hardly any roads in what is now four hundred and twelve square miles. As late as the 1880s, Leslie County was mainly forest and accessible by canoe, horseback, and walking in all kinds of weather.

Eliza showed us a painting depicting "The Old Home Place on

Cutshin:" mother washing clothes in a kettle beneath a big tree, the well for drawing up water by hand, battin' stick for getting the clothes cleaner, mule-drawn cane mill, and the picket fence encircling the log cabin.

Electricity was a distant dream.

Eliza handed us a special gift—a postcard with a little poem written by Gladys Inhout, a Frontier Nurse of the Helforsartin Clinic. We've added it to our growing collection of tokens, which we keep close by and admire—

> *Snow and ice will soon be gone,*
> *Spring tides will be startin.*
> *Dog wood trees will be in bloom*
> *All down Helforsartin.*
>
> *Mountain waters rushing clear*
> *Song birds swiftly dartin.*
> *Little rainbows in the sky*
> *over Helforsartin.*
>
> *Tears unbidden dim my eyes*
> *At the thought of partin.*
> *When I'm far away outside,*
> *I'll dream of Helforsartin.*

Hooten Holler

Here's the thing about Hooten Holler. It's a real place, a certified, card-carrying neck of the woods. The bandy-shanked man who rules the roost there, sixty-nine-year-old Ralph W. Marcum, is as real as they come. He has solid white hair, a twinkle in his eye, and a bounce in his hip-and-hurry step.

Ralph can squint at a piece of wood and carve it into something useful, and he can swap yarns six ways from Sunday.

Ralph's home of homes is Hooten Old Town on Hooten Branch about a mile up a gravel road, about two miles off KY 89 in Jackson County. If you get to Hurley you've gone a smack dab too far. Collect yourself, spud around, and go back apace.

Best not go unannounced in the middle of the night. "If I don't know you, I'm not home," says Ralph, a believer in the old idee that a man's home is his castle—or his grist mill—or just his squattin'-down place.

"I'll have a good old time if nobody comes but me," says Ralph, whittling a piece of cedar and speaking of the mid-summer Hooten Old Town Antique Power Show—"Bring your antique engines, grist mills, tractors, cars, & trucks, for a day of old time fun and fellowship."

The thing about Ralph, he doesn't charge admission. The other thing about him, he's a walking, talking medical marvel. Six and a half years ago the doctors removed his stomach, gall bladder, spleen, and part of his pancreas.

"I went in weighing one hundred and fifty-five and three months later I was one hundred and eight." Using five inches of his small intestine, the surgeon jury-rigged Ralph a new stomach, and now he's now back up to one hundred and thirty pounds of lively energy. He moves as fast as any varmint up Wildcat Holler.

Hooten Holler Old Town looks like a movie set: blacksmith shop, saloon, gallows, jail, church, funeral parlor; buggies, stage coach, 1856 printing press, photography shop; original grist mill, water mill, and a "good dog" named Dolly.

As a woman once said in a doctor's office, "Rather have a good dog than a man."

"You don't have it, it has you," says Ralph, the mayor, governor, and president of Hooten Holler. His first lady Mertie works daytime at the Jackson Energy (Rural Electric Cooperative) office in McKee. After hours she goes to Hooten Holler to cook, clean up, and check on her buzz saw, Ralph.

Ralph Marcum's careers include twenty-six years as a featured fiddler at Renfro Valley, twenty-seven years as a schoolteacher and since his operation, editor and publisher of the *Hooten Old Town Epitaph.*

This phantom elf of the Daniel Boone National Forest is a civil war reenactment buff who rides a horse named "Buck" and is available as a Confederate or a Yankee, take your pick—Morgan's Second Kentucky horse drawn CSA Artillery or First Kentucky Cavalry horse drawn US Artillery—it don't make no never mind.

Once a day, Ralph goes up to Sand Gap to check on his parents in their nineties—"Just me being a good fellow," says Ralph with no resemblance to the old 'Lil Abner stereotype. What furriner Al Capp did to God-fearin' Kentuckians, especially Appalachian Kentuckians, was a misdeed that should have been punished. That feller should've been tarred and feathered and sent back to wherever he come from.

Standing alongside Hooten Branch at the headwaters of the middle fork of Rockcastle River is something like being in a different time, B.A.C. (Before Al Capp)—the 1880s or thereabouts—and somehow it feels natural and reassuring to be there. Nothing was perfect then, of course, any more than now, one hundred and twenty-five years later. But, there's quality time to be spent off the main road from Sand Gap to McKee, and it has a certain way of making you forget your troubles—whether it be poor health, road rage, televised tabloid, or just too many dern bills to pay.

Ralph Marcum and we get worn out with folks complaining about every little thing from prostate meltdown to macular degeneration. So, we agree to meet again, not to talk about our aches and pains, but rather to enjoy for the sake of enjoyment. That would include taking a slow stroll along the wooden sidewalk past Buffalo Bull Hotel & Opera House, Forks of Wildcat Trade Co., Oregon Trail Outfitters, and Judge Roy Bean's The Jersey Lilly.

We'll set aside our modern duds and dress up the old time way. Mainly, we won't worry about tomorrow. We'll take a healthy swig of yesterday, relax, and mellow down to now.

Bozo and Horny

This is the true story of Bozo and Horny.

They were two respectable characters who've passed on now but live in a different time and place—the spiritual world of the goodhearted beasts, you might say.

Bozo lived on the edge of Morefield in the Licking River Valley in Nicholas County. Horny made her home near Gravel Switch, where the knobs of Boyle, Casey, and Marion Counties join at the hips, where North Rolling Fork flows and sings.

Bozo was born a bull calf on a Sunday morning about the time Robert and Nell Poline had dressed for church. When they looked to the pasture and saw what was happening, they quickly changed clothes and went to see if they could help, but there's only so much human beings can do at such crucial moments.

Bozo's mother died at the birthing despite their efforts, so Robert and Nell carried the newborn to the barn and began to bottle-feed him. The rest of the herd had been sold because of a brucellosis scare, but Bozo became one of God's special creatures—he'd not be sold at any price.

Bozo was neutered, and he grew up to weigh two thousand pounds. He became a downright grateful member of the family. When Robert went on his early evening walks, the gentle animal would always be waiting for the master's return—a magical meeting of the minds in the shiny bucket of sweet feed.

They say, Bozo could have become a champion, but you know how that goes: a blue ribbon leading to an unceremonious date with the butcher.

No, not that!

The friendly brute with the big eyes just moseyed around the farm for twelve good years. The inevitable day would dawn—Bozo went to sleep peacefully and did not wake up. Robert and Nell buried their friend as close as possible to the spot where he was born that distant Sunday.

Then there was the cow named Horny.

She got her name from the way her horns grew out in a nice curve and then came together so that from the front it looked like a diadem, a crowning bovine statement.

Jeanne Penn Lane, present proprietor of the famous Penn's Store, the oldest continuously owned and operated store (by the same family) in the United States, estimates that Horny lived to be an incredible thirty-eight years.

"I stopped by the hayshed (as I always do when I leave out) to give Horny a bucket of feed...if sitting down she would struggle to get up and wobble over to eat. To view her from the rear was like looking at a heart with hooves being the apex."

Jeanne hurried to town to run her errands, then came home as quickly as possible. She gave Horny another opportunity to take a taste from the sweet feed bucket, but the grand old lady wanted no part of it.

"So, I petted Horny and let her know what a wonderful Queen she had been to the herd and farm. She looked at me and I KNEW."

Jeanne decided she couldn't afford to pay to put Horny down, so she just asked the "Powers That Be" to decide the time, which came soon enough.

"Bruce Crain is coming in the morning with his backhoe to dig the grave behind the hayshed," Jeanne wrote. "It has saddened me...she made it through the winter...I know all the locals thought I was 'wacky' putting Horny up the past two winters...carrying her water and feed every day...through ice and snow and subzero temps. But she was royalty to me and had served the herd and farm all these years, had many wonderful calves who had helped keep the farm going and it was my turn to honor that."

Jeanne decided to plant a garden over Horny's grave.

A wise old farmer once warned, it's a danger to give animals names, to anthropomorphize them by assigning human characteristics to them. Yet, humans sometimes behave in bestial ways and the dividing line is blurred between physical and spiritual.

That's the way this story ends, fresh flowers and green grass growing.

Jewell Box

There's a Jewell Box we'd like to tell you about.

It's not exactly fancy, not overdone, or fussy.

We found it by the side of the road in Hart County at the Jonesboro crossroads eleven and a half miles south of Hodgenville on U.S. 31E. Or, if you were to back track from Munfordville, it would be about ten or eleven and a half miles, depending on which raveling road you've amind to take.

Doris Jewell and her daughter, Zelda Gammons, were all smiles when we settled down to getting better acquainted. The telephone rang every once in a while and customers came quietly in, now and again, but mostly we were able to enjoy the Jewell Box until right on to closing time.

You see, the Jewell Box is one of those alternative crops that actually works—neither peppers, Christmas trees, goats, nor artichokes. Well, maybe the aforementioned have been agricultural cat's meows for a few, but Doris Jewell and daughter Zelda prefer a different way of skinning a stubborn, whiskered creature.

Doris and her husband Ray (they married when she was fifteen and he was seventeen, which was forty-four years ago) live in Round Bottom Bend, where Green River loops so tightly back on itself, getting there reminds one of threading a needle.

Ray's school bus driving helps the farming squeeze too, no question about it, but it's the Jewell Box that spells an extra helping of financial cents and sense for the family.

"He says it's a hobby, but he loves it," says Doris about Ray while he's out making his daily bus run for the little darlings. He still remembers the day a youngster bloodied his nose (Ray's), knocked out a tooth, and "loosened all in front."

It was six years ago that Doris hitched up her courage and bought a fabric shop after its owner had died. She and her daughter moved it out to the main highway where a long time ago there'd been a general store. Now there are three floors with an upholstery shop in the basement where a sign reads: "If you are grouchy or just plain mean there will be a $40 charge for putting up with you."

The prices at The Jewell Box are often close to half what they'd be in Louisville, and the customer gets plenty of friendly, ungrouchy service thrown in.

"You want to please people, and we try to have a little bit of everything," says Zelda, who lives on another farm with her husband and children. There's a seventeen-year-old daughter, who wants to be an artist like her mother, and a fourteen-year-old son, who "piddles with the sewing machine. He likes the gears."

Doris and Zelda are a team that knows the meaning of long hours and Kentucky ingenuity handed down through generations. "Both grandmothers sewed. One did fancy, one was more utility. Keep my nose buried in here six days a week. Not sure which one of us is the sidekick. It's not mine and it's not hers. We're more settled in to what we're doing. So much to do, Don't have time to teach classes—we've learned by doing by the seat of our pants. Takes two together (farm and fabric.)

Any advice?

"Stay healthy. Be happy in what you do. Always keep learning about what you're interested in. Go with the flow."

The Jewell Box is a treasure house of wall-to-wall, floor-to-ceiling quilts, quilts, and more quilts ("we're thirty quilts behind") and a "long arm quilting machine in the basement," which came from Louisville in a cattle trailer. Zelda and her sister, Cathy Rock, went up there in a hurry, bought the expensive machinery, and brought it home to Green River country, where "lots of tourists are traveling the side roads, looking for quilting shops. People buy more than they make. Not as many people sewing as once did."

There's also a goodly supply of recovered pillows, flowered ironing board covers, painted handsaws, old fashioned dolls, baby quilts, laced notions, spools and spools of thread, needles and tools, custom sewing, wedding things, alterations, automobile headliners, and yards and yards and yards of fabrics, seasonal fabrics all the time, "No idea how many bolts," says Zelda.

Now, you can have your cows, your heifers and your calves, your tobacco, corn and hay, and the derned river that comes along whenever it takes a crazy-butted notion to take out your fence, and you can have your rambunctious, freewheeling school bus platoons, Doris and Zelda have found a higher, dryer, safer place for a successful family business by the side of the road.

They call it The Jewell Box.

Winery

High upon a hill in Henry County, the chickens are gone and the milk cows are gone, but there's plenty happening.

As they said in that movie about baseball and unconventional cornfields, build it and they'll come.

About eight thousand visited the new Berry-Smith winery since August of last year. There had to be a reason for it. As that old farmer once said as he surveyed his fields: Son, it don't just happen. Somebody works hard to make it happen.

When we stopped by the winery this summer, we were greeted by Mary Berry Smith, who happens to be Wendell and Tanya Berry's daughter. Although he's internationally acclaimed as an author—*The Memory of Old Jack, Jaber Crow,* and *What are People For?* —most Henry Countians think of him and his extended family as good neighbors and dedicated farmers. They're conservationists with a bumper crop of imagination, enthusiasm, and one of the finest states of mind.

This story is about Mary, but it wouldn't be complete without praise for her husband, Chuck. He said he understood and went on with his chores. After he was gone, Mary said, "He's a born entrepreneur," who won't give up on something 'until it works.'"

So.

We stay awhile in the converted 1890 buggy shed, which is presently the tasting room. It's located in the large backyard of the Smith residence.

"It's a building we always loved," said Mary.

Two dogs sleeping by the front door barely raised their heads when company arrived, and it was apparent that they knew their boundaries.

The Smiths used to have a chicken processing operation, but it turned out to be more feathers than they'd anticipated. Droughts didn't help the organic vegetables venture. The market didn't sustain the dairy project (a nice way of saying life's too short to dance with shitty milk cows, twice a day, 365 days a year).

Five years ago, Mary and Chuck took a trip to California. While they were there they visited the Napa Valley region. They spent time at an eight-acre vineyard. Asked questions. Got answers.

Made up their own minds.

"That's eight acres of tobacco," said Chuck, realizing that there is life after tobacco, not to mention chickens and dairy cows. Maybe grapes would work. Maybe quality wine would fill Kentucky bottles just as well as California bottles. Maybe people would drive to Henry County and experience a difference in a project with an unusual touch.

Chuck and Mary returned to Kentucky and successfully campaigned in a local option election, making it legal for them to grow grapes, process them in the now cow-less dairy barn, and sell bottles of fine wine over the counter— individual to individual, smile to smile.

Since it's not legal for the Smiths to ship so much as one bottle of wine anywhere, people find their way to the little winery on top of the hill just outside New Castle. They take away a breath of fresh air and maybe a sense of being closer to the fruit of the good earth.

"Quality matters so much," says Mary.

But, it's not just wine. Neither is it Napa Valley. It's Kentucky and Kentuckians working hard to win approval.

The Smith-Berry acreage is a place for wedding receptions, outdoor concerts, catered meals at a long table where cows used to line up and the milking machines used to hum. Mary, the chef, laughs today and wonders what the cows would moo of the art exhibits on the walls.

Why make such an investment of money and time, a skeptic might wonder?

There are three daughters—ages twenty-three, twenty, and fifteen—and Mary and Chuck are hopeful that one day there'll be something of real value to pass down to the next generation and the ones after that.

A place to come to.

A home where what you sell is what you make.

"What can we do here to keep our children here?" asks Mary, then answers her own question.

"We want to have something here for them," she says. The vineyard, the winery, and the converted buggy shed speak volumes.

"Who's going to do it?" Mary asks, but this answer remains unspoken. It's a given, at least it seems so. Mary and Chuck will do it. After they are gone, their daughters and their grandchildren will follow.

And they will do it.

Mary shares a bit of economic/agricultural/community philosophy: "It's dangerous for a country if everybody works for somebody else."

It's an idea worth considering. Maybe it won't work for everybody all the time, but if it'll work for some of us some of the time, that should be a crown worth wearing in a society needing the best each one of us has to offer.

Straw Bale House

"Be sure and dress warmly because though we have electric we do not have the heating system up and running…happy to see you have an intelligent view of what we are doing. Some of the local people think we are a little weird.

"All it is is a lack of knowledge."

So wrote the Abshires (Terry is the woman of the house-to-be, Kirty is the husband). From their building site in the Johnson Creek woods of Robertson County, their voices are a clear call for individuality, pure grit, and lots of imagination.

Our paths first crossed on a nippy November Sunday, and we haven't been the same since. You see, we'd never heard of a "straw-bale house."

You could say, we were raised up on the silly old fairy tale about the critters that built their house out of straw and, guess what? The bad old wolf came along and blew and blew and blew the house down.

Well, any bad old wolves would have their fangs full trying to blow down the Abshire home in the year 2005. The walls are over eighteen inches thick.

According to Catherine Wanek, who has written on the subject of straw-bale homes, "In the 1890s, pioneers of the sand hills of

Nebraska found themselves building a new life on a treeless prairie, and from necessity began building their homes from bales of straw. Now modern day pioneers are choosing straw bale construction for its many advantages—for people and the planet."

Seeing, feeling, and touching are the better parts of believing, so we set out for Robertson County. With David driving, and with me navigating, we decided an open state of mind was the best way to go.

Two of the welcomers were dogs, Annie and Ladybug. Then came homebuilders Terry and Kirty along with Eugene (he's got a million-dollar smile and a determination uncommon in a twenty-six-year-old).

The house is more than just straw bales.

Hand-hewn cedar poles. Almost two thousand square feet of living space, great room, three bedrooms, each with full bath, and an eighty-pound limestone door stop carved in the form of a turtle.

Terry is especially proud of what will become her kitchen, although it hasn't quite taken shape. She had her choice as to whether she would face east or west while standing at the sink.

"I chose the sunset," she says.

Then there's the "truth window." That's for the benefit of any doubters that in the middle of three coats of concrete, inside and out, there's the friendship of straw bales in place of artificial insulation—a glassed-in peephole to the heart of the matter, if you will.

The Abshires say their house is "built around windows." It seemed the better aesthetic approach.

In fact, the house was begun before a plan, sort of like driving down a road and then making a map. This might be a little upsetting to the architectural/navigational crowd, but there's a whole lot to be said for dreaming a dream, and then going to work to make it happen.

"It's how our mind works," say the Abshires. "We rented a backhoe and dug the footers."

Seven years later, the electrical work is almost finished, the straw bales are neatly pummeled into place, smoothed off with a little help from a weed eater, and it's time for the final concrete and drywall work.

Then there's the tile to be fitted along with carpet.

Resist the temptation to think the straw bales are a fire hazard. Actually, it has a better fire rating than other material, and it's all according to code. And how about an insulation "R rating" of over sixty with a savings of over seventy-five percent of heating and cooling costs?

No fireplace, but "...totally handicap accessible, one floor, a labor of love," says Terry, but maybe it was Kirty. He calls it your "basic disabled-Vietnam-veteran-low-income house. We've done everything but the roof ourselves."

Kirty's father may come from Texas to live in the straw bale house that sits on top of a ridge. If he doesn't make it, the Abshires already have the elder's handprint set in concrete to place in the wall. There're lots of surprises like that in the house that chooses to defy conventionality.

Call it "alternative housing"—the Abshires sold their tobacco base in order "to get started—to build the foundation. People said we were crazy for doing that." But they did it, and they may have the last laugh.

Terry, whose roots are in Casey County but who was born in Cincinnati, and Kirty, who was born in Crowley, Louisiana, are of one mind: "We always wanted to be in Kentucky."

So they settled on a high ridge overlooking Robertson County. "It's been our dream of a lifetime," says Terry.

Soon the dream will be completed.

"By next winter we'll be in."

Gourds

Across the Ohio River from Stephensport in Breckinridge County, Kentucky, a child was born May 3, 1973, in the little community of Rome, Indiana.

Her name is Jennifer and her passion is gourds, gourds, and more gourds.

The best news of all is that she moved to within fifteen miles from Plum Lick, and now we're ten gourd seeds richer.

You can be too. We'll tell you how it could work a little later in the story, but for now let us tell you some more about the amazing young woman who takes a plain, ordinary gourd and turns it into art as fine as anything you'll ever see.

Jennifer Zingg is twenty-nine years old, and she likes to say, "Art is fearlessness...you learn from doing...if you fail you go on to the next step...I don't think with one thing...I want to do mentorships with kids. (That's part of the reason why Jennifer's ten-year-old son, Logan, is an avid arrowhead collector.)

Did you know that there are hundreds of varieties of gourds?

From dippers to bird houses. And there we were thinking a gourd is a gourd is a gourd. No way.

There're the "bushel basket" gourd for creating bowls, the "Calabash" gourd for making pipes out of curved stems, the "egg" gourd, the "canteen" gourd, and the "longneck dipper" gourd for scooping up drinking water on a hot summer's day. Purple martins have been known to prefer gourd birdhouses.

It doesn't take long to move past birdhouses to the eternal land of art by gourd. One of Jennifer's favorites is her "Curley-Tailed Crazy Cat." Others are her "Tulip Bowl" and "Cactus Flower." She says she prefers natural things with humble beginnings.

There are gourd farmers who plant their seed in summer and harvest in fall, but we're not advocating this as another alternative crop. Let's just call it amateur gourdsmanship—a simple activity involving a child of nature (the unassuming gourd), and a willingness to have fun and be creative (that's us).

It's true, Jennifer Zingg has elevated the lowly gourd to works of art commanding prices ranging from fifty to four hundred dollars. But, no, that's not the point.

Growing gourds can be good for several of the five senses. Shapes are symmetrical and pleasant to behold and they're smooth to the touch. They're relaxing to hear when made into "rain sticks." But— let's be honest—there are better things to taste and smell (although properly dried and handled, the mustiness can be cured, and I suppose, a survivalist could turn a gourd into something to chew for a little while.)

Jennifer tells us that the first thing she does is to remove the gourd from the vine and let it dry. Turn it occasionally for a season or two. If you open the gourd, save the seeds. Work carefully with a sander and seal with paint. That ought to take care of the smell, but remember that mold and mustiness give the creature its character. Maybe that's why the purple martins like it.

There's plenty of good gourd information on the Internet. We typed in "Gourds Kentucky" and came up with 2,628 opportunities, including the "Kentucky Gourd Society," which has a newsletter and a web site that tells how to become a member.

Are you old enough to remember Allan Trout, the columnist for *The Courier-Journal*? His "Greetings!" appeared 8,988 times and the noble gourd was not left out. He used this cousin of the pumpkin, squash, and cucumber as a way of connecting people. If it takes a gourd to do it, that's reward and reason enough to be involved.

In case you don't have access to the Internet, you're invited to send to us your gourd ideas, your gourdiest thoughts, your successes and your failures. From time to time, we might be able to swap some gourd seed: Kentucky's most unusually shaped gourd, memories of gourds gone by, new gourds for a new day!

Baskets

...and they took up of the fragments that remained twelve baskets full.

In order for the miracle to have occurred, according to St. Matthew, there had to have been twelve basket makers. This means flexible reeds, nimble hands, and long traditions pre-dating corrugated boxes and coopers' tools.

Before there were barrels and stainless steel bins, there were basket makers.

The tradition lives today with the Bluegrass Basket Makers who again this June will sponsor a Basket Seminar at Lake Cumberland, where there's more to life than just boats.

C'mon down! Or up. Or sideways. Weave yourself in!

This annual get-together is sponsored by Bluegrass Area Extension Homemakers and will last for four days at the Kentucky Leadership Center at Jabez, Kentucky.

Registration is first come, first served and the last day for registration is in early May, although the classes are filling rapidly. Registration fee is around thirty dollars. Class descriptions and meal and lodging information may be obtained from your local extension office. Keep in mind that the cost of learning basket weaving at the seminar could range from twelve to one hundred and fifty-five dollars.

"The basket seminar is for dedicated basket makers," writes Cheryl Case, Harrison County Extension Agent for Family & Consumer Sciences at the University of Kentucky College of Agriculture. "Classes are designated as beginner, intermediate and advanced levels and are limited to twelve per class."

You may attend the seminar for one day or for all four days.

We homemakers competing in a time of agricultural uncertainty understand that nothing plus nothing equals not much. The registration fee for learning to weave fine baskets is about what we'd spend for a meal for two at many restaurants. Let's not even talk about the price of gasoline, tractors, or pickup trucks.

At the same time, there're no guarantees, few miracles, and no free lunches when it comes to learning the ins and outs of such creations as "Nature's Bounty," "Baby's First Wagon," "Fancy Oval Egg Basket," "Simplicity," and "Harmony"—just a few of the many class projects to be undertaken at this year's workshop.

Consider this: Yvonne Summers of Estill County has been a frequent attendee at the Basketmakers Seminar. "She now has her own business," says Bourbon County Extension Agent for Family and Consumer Sciences Betty K. Overly.

Yvonne has been invited to teach in two states as a result of being featured as 'Entrepreneur of the Year' at the 2001 seminar. "Learning new techniques has inspired me to create designer baskets using my hobby of collecting antlers," says Yvonne.

This year's faculty of twenty-four is a who's who of basket making representing Florida, Indiana, Kentucky, Michigan, Missouri, Ohio, North Carolina, Texas, West Virginia, Wisconsin, and as far away as Canada.

Susan Coyle of Menasha, Wisconsin, began weaving baskets in 1977. She calls it a "stress reliever." In other words, you don't have to be a basket case in order to be a basket maker, but it may make sense to become a basket maker before becoming a basket case. (Free advice, according to Dr. Lalie.)

Not everybody is going to become an entrepreneur, teacher, innovator, or do-it-yourself cornfield psychologist, but sometimes the results can be pretty amazing. According to Betty Overly, one participant has estimated that in one year she has supplemented the family income by eight thousand dollars. "Two participants indicated that they had saved four hundred dollars per year in purchases of ready-made baskets for themselves or as gifts."

Knox County Extension Service Agent Terena Edington has told of the 1999 Basket Retreat: "It is estimated that over 163 baskets were made and given as gifts at a value of $6,846.00."

Another basket maker was quoted as saying, "Families take pride receiving a piece of hand-made art." Now there's a Christmas or birthday idea. Bad news for the stores, good news for those who want to do it "their way."

In a time of "alternative crops" the ancient and not-so-ancient art of basket making could take its rightful place in the challenging days ahead on the farm, which could be a good argument for not putting all our eggs in one basket.

Baskets made by mother, grandmother or great-grandmother have become as prized as handmade quilts, homegrown painted gourds, or hand carved walking sticks.

Some important items that can be tucked down in your basket and taken away from this seminar are personal touch, quality outcome, deep satisfaction of achievement, and the knowledge that you are continuing an age-old tradition.

Puttin' in the Love

Cooking Tip #1: "Don't forget to put in the love. Otherwise, it's just food."

Words set on the wall of the kitchen of the Baptist Student Center at Eastern Kentucky University are more than just a promise. It constitutes a mission statement going straight to the heart of Home Meals Delivery.

"Makes you feel good," say the cooks, Ona French and Donna Masters.

From early in the morning to midday, they stir the pots and fill the boxes for approximately sixty needy recipients in Richmond.

"Makes you feel special going on each delivery, meeting people and seeing their faces," says Donna.

Syble Miller coordinates the Monday through Friday schedule, providing 16,000 meals a year. "It is astounding!

"It takes ten volunteers each day to deliver four routes to sixty individuals. These volunteers are from all areas of our community: civic groups, churches, EKU, fraternities and sororities, EKU Baptist Student Union and individuals. A board member volunteers to coordinate all of these people."

For twenty-five consecutive years, this steadfast, dedicated work of Home Meals Delivery, a non-profit, volunteer service to the Richmond community, has filled a fundamental necessity.

Unselfish volunteerism has made a positive difference in the lives of people, often alone and unable to prepare balanced meals for themselves.

The criteria is NEED.

Hardly anything could be simpler or clearer. Hardly anything could be more beneficial and fulfilling. Unstructured by bureaucracy, rigid job descriptions or hidden agendas of any kind, Home Meals Delivery is the work of angels.

Stardust becomes hot spaghetti!

Unfolded heavenly wings become chicken and salmon, baked beans, and Salisbury steak.

Where there's a need, there's a way to meet it, and it's no time for playing favorites. We're all a part of the food chain of humanity.

"We do not discriminate on the grounds of race, color, national origin, age, sex, or disability," says Syble Miller, herself recovering from a sight disorder, which has not slowed her down or lessened her enthusiasm or prevented her from seeing a bigger, brighter picture.

"We have too many blessings to complain. Many food recipients are diabetic, as many as one-third...some are young and disabled... some see nobody but us...."

Recipients may sign up for temporary delivery, while they're recovering from illness or injury.

Each situation is evaluated according to the individual need with a small fee for each person's ability to pay—a top cost of two dollars and fifty cents for a hot, nutritious meal delivered to the door, rain or shine, snow or no snow.

Each Thanksgiving is an extra special occasion, when "there's a mountain of canned foods to be sorted and it's almost impossible to count the number of volunteers, who map it all out....There are three-to four-hundred meals to be prepared and delivered.

There's even one ninety-year old woman who volunteers to snap the beans.

"In the summer, individuals volunteer to help in the food preparation of fresh vegetables that have been donated. Volunteers pick up the fruit and vegetables four days a week and bring them to the center. Two days a week, a volunteer picks up donuts that have been donated by the local donut shop. A volunteer licensed electrician does needy work for us free. Fifteen board members volunteer their time for monthly board meetings to oversee the program.

"It's a community effort...Several churches have us in their budget...Boy Scouts are involved...Mail carriers have their annual canned food campaigns...Service organizations are active in the program...Individuals make donations of food and cash....

"God has had his hand in it...We're all God's children."

It seems only right that Home Meals Delivery of Richmond began a quarter of a century ago in a local fish market, where a modern-day version of fishes and loaves flourished and grew to become such substantial bread in one of God's Kentucky communities.

For anyone wishing to help, here are some names and numbers—

Financial contributions, which are tax-deductible, may be made payable to Home Meals Delivery, c/o Baptist Student Center, Eastern Kentucky University, Richmond, Kentucky 40475. Individuals or groups who would like to help with delivery or other volunteer jobs can contact the Center at 623-3294 between 8:00 a.m. and 12 p.m. weekdays or call 623-8446.

On the other hand, come to think of it, maybe you'd be interested in establishing your own volunteer organization in one of the other one hundred and nineteen counties in Kentucky.

It could be as simple as knowing the need in the home next door.

Remember, though, Cooking Tip #1:

"Don't forget to put in the love. Otherwise, it's just food."

Kate and Other Sisters

David has several collections—ties he's never worn, books he's not had the time to read, and five lifelike nuns in ceramics.

They are Sister Mary Praises, Sister Mary Hubert, Sister Mary Paprika, Sister Mary Leo, and Sister Mary Guidance—all dressed in traditional habit, something you don't see much anymore.

Sister Mary Paprika is holding a kettle of stew in her right hand and a large wooden spoon in the left. Sister Mary Leo is living dangerously with ballet slippers showing beneath her flowing, black gown. Sisters Mary Praises and Mary Hubert appear like cheerleaders for the group, while in front stands Mary Guidance with two leather-bound books cradled on her left arm and a large red apple in her extended right hand.

Sister Mary Guidance is the older nun, right after Sister Paprika.

Which brings us to our encounter this summer past with Sister Kate from, of all places, David, Kentucky.

Sister Kate is no ceramic.

She's real, and we'd like to tell you about her.

First of all, her name is actually Sr. Kathleen Weigand, and she's one of six nuns who live at the Benedictine Sisters of the Dwelling Place Monastery on Mt. Tabor Road near Martin, in Floyd County.

Sr. Kate, as we like to call her, is a native of Pittsburgh, Pennsylvania. Now, she's a Kentuckian, and she's here to stay—permanence of place being one of her vows as a Benedictine.

Each of the nuns at the monastery, perched high on a hill, dedicates her life to some need in nearby communities. Sister Kate is Executive Director of St. Vincent Mission in David, Kentucky. It's located on Hwy 404, six miles from Rt. 114, which is the eastern extension of the Bert T. Combs Mountain Parkway. There's a sign pointing to David, and you probably won't miss it.

Traveling with David to a place called David, we're sorry to say, is an ego trip for him. But, for the rest of us, it's simply worth the effort.

You'd probably not know Sister Kate is a nun, unless you asked. In which case, she might reply, "Why sure." To sit with her and members of her staff in the crafts room of St. Vincent Mission is to be enveloped in craftsmanship paradise. There's just about everything from quilts to tobacco sticks turned into walking canes. Business is brisk, because the word has gone out that something pretty wonderful is happening here.

The Mission Statement includes this idea: "In Appalachia, working together, we become enriched and strengthened by a common respect. Through concrete programs we encourage the use of our skills, talents, and personal gifts to help each other. Our Mission is one of HOPE that leads us toward a vision of continuous growth."

To put real life into the project and achieve positive results, there's a secondhand store or "David Boutique" to help low income families purchase "used clothing or household items at a reasonable price."

And there's a Christmas Store "for families who would otherwise have little nor nothing for Christmas." Sister Kate wants the world outside to know that "donations of new clothes, toys, and money are solicited throughout the year by the Mission staff in preparation for distribution in mid-December. Invitations are sent to the most needy families in the area in early December. When parents arrive to select Christmas gifts for their family they are asked to donate two dollars to the mission and participate in budget counseling."

There's a project for helping to repair homes, a summer youth program, and there's a scholarship fund for needy students.

St. Vincent Mission is a non-profit (501 (c) 3) corporation, making gifts tax-deductible.

The postal address is: St. Vincent Mission, P.O. Box 232, David, Kentucky 41616. (No, David, you can't have your own personal zip code. So, behave.)

You can have a catalog for David Appalachian Crafts by sending $2.00 to David Appalachian Crafts, P.O. Box 2, David, Kentucky 41616.

A final word or two about ceramic nuns in traditional garb, however clever, is not quite the same thing as a real-life nun like Sister Kate.

In this year's spring issue of *Mt. Tabor News*, Sr. Kathleen wrote: "The personal aspect of poverty is perhaps the most compelling reason for each of us to become actively involved. Our lives are changed as we journey together. If you want to make a difference you have to make a start, right where you are."

Thanksgiving

With hands folded in prayer, with mind clear of worry, and with heart beating in calm assurance—in each month of thanksgiving—we use these pages of our lives to give thanks.

First, we give thanks for the miracle of life, knowing that in this slender window of time—without fancy and expensive shutters, streaked by many rains and flakes of snow—we have an opportunity to give back all that we've received.

Then, we're beholden to our soul mate—for David's wife Lalie, for her loyalty and her wisdom. For Lalie's husband David for his patience and persistence. We do not know how such a blueprint for joy could have been designed more wonderfully. We just don't doubt God's master plan.

We give thanks for our children and stepchildren, and our grand- and step-grandchildren, and we want each one to know how proud we are to have been a part of their miraculous creation. We have a strong belief in generational flow and forward movement.

Before this sounds too much like a last will and testament, we want to speak to your miracles of Thanksgivings past—you know, the ones when the family gathered to feast on turkey and dressing, fried chicken, old ham and beaten biscuits, tomato aspic, cornbread, corn pudding, scalloped oysters, and pecan pie with a big dip of vanilla ice cream sliding around on top of it.

"How about this baby boy and this baby girl growing up so fast?"

"To tell you the truth, seems like only yesterday that we came home from the hospital."

"Hospital, my foot! In my time we had 'em at home, first squall to goin' off time!"

"Go on yourself, Grandma, didn't you take a vacation and have to be brought home in a stretch limousine?"

"Pshaw!"

We are grateful for the laughter of long ago voices because without it we'd be living in a desolate dust storm. After laughter might come a smile where there hadn't been one before.

Yes, there are those imprisoned, impoverished, or disenfranchised who've suffered lonely Thanksgiving Days. Every prayer should include hope and help for those who have little or nothing.

A list of other precious things deserving a handwritten note of appreciation: fresh air to breathe, clouds filled with rain, pure water to drink, sunshine, and leather-bound books to read.

Teachers!

Surely it's time to revisit a teacher in a nursing home, especially those who should've cracked our knuckles, but didn't.

Doctors!

Remember the ones who made house calls? All those who didn't bungle the surgery? Those assistants who emptied the bedpans, and those who wheeled you out to the waiting car?

Preachers!

Remember those who were always there when they were needed most? Those who knew when to stop preaching and simply hold your hand?

Even politicians! Especially those who are honestly dedicated to the public's need. There are many deserving of our votes every election month.

Imagine the power we hold in our fingertips when we enter the November voting booth and touch the names of those to whom we've decided to grant our favor and legitimate expectation.

November 11, is Veterans' Day in the United States. Dare we not disremember those who've given their lives that we might live in freedom guaranteed by the First Amendment.

November is the special month set aside for giving many kinds of thanks, but every month should be a time for gratitude. Saying "thank you" has too often gone the way of saying "excuse me" and "I'm sorry for the hurt I may have caused."

Thanksgiving is a time for selecting a special log of locust for the fire on the hearth of another approaching winter. It is a time for folded hands with finger tips lightly touching the lips of anticipation.

It is a time for prayer.

Warmth

We decided to begin the New Year with a second wood-burning stove. Thought it made good sense and cents to kick the addiction to fuel oil consumption. We'd heard all the warnings about skyrocketing prices, and we decided it might even be patriotic to round up the chain saw, sledgehammer, and steel wedges and lay in a supply of wood for the winter of 2006.

As for 2005, we'd accept the offer of a neighbor who had a barn full of seasoned locust, black walnut, and Osage orange, which he said was waiting for our pickup truck to be sent in his direction. No charge!

Call it God's gift to the cold and shivering.

We've come a long way since the fire at the mouth of the cave, but it's well to remember that wood-burning stoves don't fall out of the sky. There's work and work and there's saving and saving, then the possibility of sharing the overage.

Another neighbor, not to be outdone, deposited a pile of the inedible Osage orange wood on the doorstep of our coal house, and he departed with not so much as a "here's a little something for your new stove."

It took three grown men to install the take-no-prisoners critter designed to keep us warm on three-dog nights. First, the mainly ornamental grate had to be removed (make an interesting flower pot come Spring), and there needed to be a steel sleeve inserted into the stone chimney to provide a good draft and, we hope, keep this old house from burning down.

The first load of seasoned wood, split to fit inside the firebrick-lined contraption, was brought home with as much celebration as winning the World Series. Logs stacked nicely on the back porch/mudroom lent a welcomed measure of windbreak for the outside dogs, Pumpkin and Kink. They and we could tell right off, a woodchopper is blessed with extra-added features not commonly associated with expensive fuel oil and impersonal furnace technology.

Part of the first load of timber found a resting-place in the circular container near the side porch door, a handy repository for kindling and other stray pieces of softwood. Fires, like relationships, start much better when handled delicately at the start, then given a chance to warm up for later fulfillment.

The sledgehammer and steel wedges brought back memories of younger, reckless days, but it was still possible to handle the task if patience was given a chance—split a new log down the middle, then half the halves. Good fires prefer generous surfaces with occasional splinters tenderly hanging on.

Lordy, it doesn't matter if the telephone is ringing or the fax machine is hot to trot. Digitized transmissions can find their own doghouses. Cyberspace folks can find somebody else to bug.

89

Violence on television can feed on itself. As for hackers and their sidekick spammers, they ought to be sent to the nearest woodpile.

On second thought, "No," let the woodpile be the one place where the woodsman can be left alone to do an honest afternoon's work. Let the softened hands of Autumn toughen to the rhythm of steel on steel. Let there be an armload of goodness to take to shelter for a pleasant year of seasoning.

Our coal house has become our woodshed and our fuel oil tank has become a court of desperate resort. The idea is to use our natural energy sparingly and thoughtfully, inspirational when spotting downed tree limbs better burned then hauled away in fuel-guzzling trucks.

It's hard to imagine sitting and staring at a furnace as a source for creativity. On the other hand, there's hardly anything as consoling as wood burning flames lapping up the fragrance of cedar and Osage orange.

A fire well tended is one of the noblest creations—fuel for the chilling heart and soul. Better than New Year's resolutions, it sets the tone for a different tomorrow.

The Visitor

An illusive elf by the name of Jasper P. Theopolis Spunk appeared at the breakfast table where a husband and his wife were having their usual two slices of thick bacon, one fried egg, and two cups of piping hot coffee.

Mr. Spunk climbed up into one of the empty chairs and, with no invitation, smiled and said: "I'm Jasper P. Theopolis Spunk, and I'm here to grant you three wishes, now what'll they be?"

The wife said, "I wish to know what to do about this infernal Christmas-card list. I mean, it keeps getting longer and longer. The price of postage stamps keeps getting higher and higher. Price of gasoline has jumped toward three dollars a gallon. I'm worn out with the entire business of trying to figure out the names of those to add and those to subtract. Do you have a solution to this problem, my dear sir?"

Without a moment's hesitation, Mr. Spunk declared: "Put the list into the compost heap along with the egg shells and forget it."

The wife said, "You mean send no Christmas cards this year?"

"I mean," said Jasper, "Do nothing that is going to multiply your worries. Try putting a little Christmas-card smile in your voice and a bit of twinkle in your eye the next time you see somebody walking down the street or road, as the case may be."

The husband said, "My turn!"

"Yes," said Mr. Spunk, "The second wish is yours my good man."

"May I call you Jasper?"

"Of course."

"I would like to be granted the wish for a long and healthy life for me and my wife — a cure for disease and failing eyesight."

Jasper cleared his throat, drummed a knuckle on the oak breakfast table, and said: "I have good news and bad news. However, the good may seem bad, and the bad may seem good. You will have to decide which is which."

The husband and wife stared at the sprite, who folded his arms, comfortably crossed his legs, and stared back. He said, "Both the good and the bad news are reality. Neither of you, nor I, as a matter of fact, is going to live forever inside our present bag of bones. As for a healthy life, please take into account all the years you smoked and drank and ran up and down the ridges. All right, so you didn't smoke and drink, but only ran up and down the ridges. There's a limit to everything, and if that were not so, we'd be stacked as high as a purple-tailed kite. Therefore, live each day with sobriety, pray for forgiveness, and stay out of the compost pile."

The husband and the wife sipped from their coffee cups, then put their heads together to confer as to the nature of the third and final wish.

"Take as much time as you need," said Jasper P. Theopolis Spunk, "But, on the other hand, don't take too long in your deliberations, because I have other breakfast tables to visit."

"We wish to know the meaning of the mystery of life," said the husband and wife. "How in the world did we find each other when there are so many centuries, so many paths, so many crossings?"

"Well now, this is the easy news and the difficult news. Yet, the easy may seem difficult, and the difficult may seem easy. You'll have to decide which way the wind blows."

"You mean, you don't know, isn't that right, Mr. Spunk?"

"I thought I said, it's all right to call me Jasper. But, never mind. The mystery of life resides in a single dewdrop and a single snowflake in the early days of winter. The mystery of life is in a puppy's wagging tail and a kitten's curious expression. The mystery of life is in one sip of coffee or a single taste of water."

"And?"

"The very best understanding of the miracle you call a mystery is the love you share with yourselves and all those who are lonely."

Jasper P. Theopolis Spunk vanished as quickly as he'd arrived.

PART
Two

---

*The idea is to dare to dream, put well thought-out
plans into action, stay focused, go with the flow of
earthly and spiritual life, and don't ever lose sight
of a worthy harbor.*

Mousie

$\mathcal{I}$t's no exaggeration to say, Mousie of Bath County is a genius. Nor would it be going too far to say what the world needs now are more Mousies.

Mickey need not apply.

Omer Banks "Mousie" Crouch was born the year Al Capp first published the comic strip Li'l Abner, which stamped the image of the ignorant Kentucky hillbilly on the minds of "educated" Americans. It stuck like bare feet to fly paper, one of the worst stereotypes ever perpetrated on a people.

The Beverly Hillbillies had its smash hit-and-run on national television and CBS seemed hell-bent to have a field day with what it called *The Real Beverly Hillbillies*. New Age woebegone Appalachians would be flown out to California to be treated to a mansion with maids and butlers, luxury cars, and a concrete pond or two. The national audience, ever ready for new peeping Tom entertainment, would pump up the ratings. It suggested much about viewer discretion.

We'd not be watching.

We'd rather be in the company of Mousie Crouch, youngest of ten children born to Leona Davis and Curn Crouch "way up a holler" in a three-room house with a deep fireplace and a big back log That would be on Prickley Ash Creek in the vicinity of Peasticks and White Oak Creek in Bath County.

"I like to do a man right," says Mousie as we sit and talk in his small engine repair shop in what he calls Walnut Holler, just to the north and over a couple of hills from Sharpsburg. He farmed for twenty years, "started out at two dollars and a half a day, sunup to sundown." He married Beulah Manley and they had two daughters, one who grew up to become a teacher, the other an artist. Then there were twenty years in a road contractor's shop, where Mousie was a welder and a mechanic.

The best way to describe Mousie today (or "Mouse" after you become better acquainted) is to say he's kith and kin with almost anything that has a fuel line, carburetor, cylinder, battery, and blades that turn.

"I can't fix it all, but I do my best," says Mouse as he sits "in retirement" on top of a battery charger, a recent bargain he hauled in from a tool sale. We're comfortable standing or sitting on a hay bailer seat welded to the top of a five-gallon milk can.

"I want it to be right when it goes out," says Mouse, who simply won't work on something that's past fixing. He can listen to an engine and tell you right away whether it's worth saving.

Mousey Crouch didn't make it past the sixth grade. "Geography and English didn't blend for me." He says the teachers were good, but he was more interested in numbers and how things worked and, besides, it was more than a mile walk just to get to the school bus.

The late Al Capp and CBS might choose not to believe it, but Mousie Crouch believes he has what he unashamedly calls a gift, including the natural ability to pick up a guitar, mandolin, banjo, or a Dobro and play from the bottom of his heart. The gift, not delivered until after the sixth grade, includes a patent prospect for a potato digger and a tool for removing a kitchen faucet without busting your knuckles.

Before we could leave to go back to Plum Lick, Mouse wanted to show us his two-vine grape arbor. "I think it's done better this year because of the drought. Here, taste these blue grapes." They were just right. So were the end-of-season blackberries and raspberries. So were the red delicious and yellow golden apples.

We were glad when we asked Mouse if CBS offered him a chance to go to Beverly Hills to live in a mansion and eat fancy food, he said: "I don't think I'd want to do that."

We wouldn't either.

Watchmaker

One of David's childhood fantasies was to become a watchmaker. He imagined himself hovering over shiny gears and balance stems, eyepiece gripped by his left eye socket, making adjustments that would mean the trains would run on time.

It would be a good way to focus on the work at hand without any complications—you know, not having a bunch of perfect idiots all the time telling you what to do, and how and when to do it.

After taking his first grinning Mickey Mouse watch apart and not even coming close to putting it back together again, David abandoned the idea of becoming a watchmaker, a most untimely mistake, and he moved on full steam to concentrate on becoming a barber.

He saw freshly laundered hand towels stacked just so on a handy shelf, and he could smell the conditioning solution as he worked it with his fingers through golden locks of hair. With a knowing smile, he'd accept all tips. But, something told him the part about sweeping up a floor full of golden hair might be something this side of permanent excitement.

David would be a dentist, but a little bird told him that pulling teeth would be a lot more than he could extract from his woeful bag of beginning talent.

Of the three missed callings, David would have to rank watchmaking at the top of his wish-I-had list. So, before another year was out as a reporter of human ups and downs, he decided to examine more closely what he had possibly missed.

Meet J. Don Witt of Winchester.

He's a lifelong watchmaker, born in Ford, which is located on a stretch of the Kentucky River just across from the mouth of Otter Creek. At one time, Ford was giving Winchester a run for a place in the sun, but Ford burned down in the early thirties and was never the same after that misfortune.

Before the family moved to Winchester, the mainspring of Clark County, J. Don attended a two-room school.

"Dad gave me an old dollar watch," along with "other old cheap watches," said J. Don, looking back at the time he had a book propped up in front of him at his school desk. You see, what he was studying was not what was in the book but why one of his classmate's dollar watches wouldn't run. The teach-yourself learner was using a pocketknife, and he made a miscue—watch parts flew all around like opening a bottle of fizzing pop.

The teacher wanted to know what in thunder was going on.

J. Don had to own up to the crime, while he "got down on the floor and gathered up the pieces."

At this point, some fluttering hearts might begin to think about being a barber or a dentist, but J. Don stuck with watchmaking. After the family moved to Winchester, he finagled a work permit making it legal for him to go to high school until noon, then work the rest of the day for Mr. C.A. Carruthers in his jewelry store.

Step by step, tick by tick, with each trusting customer, J. Don Witt achieved his aim in life—to be a watchmaker— which is what he is today in a tiny room on

Main Street.

"Happy man?

"Yep."

He's an individual who has learned that if you want something bad enough, chances are you'll get it. When you're in school, it doesn't pay to "goof around," unless hiding behind a book and working on a dollar watch is a case of goofing around.

J. Don Witt believes it's important to be good to yourself and good to those who need you. He's seen plenty of "goofing around" by grownups who'd have you believe they do no wrong.

As they say at the watchmaker's workbench of life, the second hand that goes around, comes around—minute hands, too.

Uncle Jed

Uncle Jed is eighty years old.

We went to see him about some herbs.

His recorded name is Roger L. Jenkins, born near Barefoot, Kentucky, close by the point where Harrison, Nicholas, and Robertson Counties come together. He attended eight grades in the one-room schoolhouse there, now vanished.

"It's along Crooked Creek about five miles downriver from Blue Licks, but it could be farther because I never measured it," says Uncle Jed, who likes to be precise about important matters.

Especially herbs.

Actually, he doesn't think of herbs as a business—he calls it his lifelong hobby. "My grandmother on my father's side, Mary Goddard— she was part Indian—she taught me about herbs from the time I was four years old."

So there you have the seed sown, which would grow up to become "Uncle Jed." We located him in his second-floor, one-room apartment, in Cynthiana —total living and working space of about three hundred square feet. Barely enough room for bed, refrigerator, microwave, copy machine, containers of dried herbs and ointments stacked to the ceiling, and shelves filled with herbal books.

"Uncle Jed, I've had radiation treatments for my ailing prostate, now I'm taking hormonal therapy for the rest of my life, do you have anything for me?"

He went to the northwest corner of the room, took down a plastic jug with a mixture of wild carrot, juniper, yellow root, cayenne, and other ingredients, and said, "Take a teaspoon of this, morning and night." Made no claims, gave no guarantees. We asked for none.

We accepted the gift with gratitude, but wondered what the medical profession would say, or the Food and Drug Administration, or the pharmaceutical industry.

"I don't prescribe," he said, "I recommend."

Directly from his grandmother and from a worn and tattered copy of Christopher's *School of Natural Healing*, Uncle Jed has taught himself to be an herbalist— "one who grows, collects, or specializes in the use of herbs, especially medicinal herbs."

We walk outside to the parking lot. Near the railroad tracks between the concrete auto bumpers and the fence, Uncle Jed has planted some of his herbs—mint, catnip, sorrel, garlic, cinnamon yam, parsley, anise, and bloodroot. The uninitiated might think somebody had neglected to annihilate the weeds, but the herbalist knows better.

Uncle Jed says it's been thirty years since he visited a doctor. Once was when a tire he was changing blew up, breaking three fingers and a bone in his face. He doesn't criticize conventional medicine, he just believes folks ought to take more personal responsibility for their health.

Some recommendations from Uncle Jed:

Watch out for sugar and fat, go real light on "heavy" meat, more fish, fresh fruit—apple a day keeps the you-know-who away, raw vegetables, whole wheat bread, little vinegar in your purified water, be careful about soft drinks, alcohol is out, so is smoking.

"Try to keep your body in balance," says Uncle Jed.

One of his remedies for what ails a body is laughter. Another thing, "money don't bother me," he says, looking back on a long life of being a mechanic for things run by motors fed by just the right mixture of fuel. He sees a parallel with the human body, its heart and moving parts.

"Don't overeat," he smiles, recalling the day he said to a farmer, "You feed minerals to your cattle don't you?"

"Of course, whenever I run out, I go and buy more."

"Well then," said Uncle Jed, "Why wouldn't you take just as good care of yourself?" The farmer shook his head in disbelief.

When we asked Uncle Jed how long he thought he might live, he had a soft-spoken answer: "As long as I'm supposed to live."

We ask if we should give out how people might contact him, and he says, "why sure."

Uncle Jed's Herbal Products, Roger L. Jenkins, Herbalist, 202 S. Walnut Street, Cynthiana, KY 41031.

Red Bird

Red Bird Mission is a jewel in the highland crown of Kentucky. For the past eighty-one years the Mission has blossomed at Beverly near the juncture of Cow Fork and Red Bird River in southern Clay County. The water and the people flow from the past through the present to the future—no perfection, but generations are striving for it.

It might be said, the promise of perfection is built on spiritual and humanitarian practice with an abundance of prayer.

Red Bird Mission, guided by Jesus Christ, empowers individuals and advocates justice by providing spiritual, educational, health and community outreach ministries. It goes without saying, any mission statement is hollow without the blood, sweat and tears of people actively engaged. So it was at Red Bird in the beginning, and so it will be at the last reckoning.

Craig Dial is one of a long line of leaders who've addressed the needs and traditions of an area often misread if read at all. He smiles—a firmly-etched smile—laughs at himself—without being a laughingstock—

listens without rushing in—no barrage of beliefs or dusty bags of theory.

As director of economic opportunities, Craig Dial breathes the essence of Appalachia. His place on the Red Bird Mission's organization chart includes Clothing and Household Assistance, Crafts and Craft Marketing.

"If you learn by what didn't work, you've learned a lot," says Craig as we sit in rocking chairs at this year's Kentucky Crafted: The Market at the Fairgrounds in Louisville. Though it's a good thing to gather once a year on common ground, there's no substitute for paying homage at the source.

Red Bird Mission is a lively place to visit. Take the Daniel Boone Parkway east from London to Manchester. You'll begin to see parts of Red Bird River, and you may wish to recall that the stream is named for Chief Red Bird, the Cherokee murdered and dumped into the water—a sobering legend to renew a more dedicated interest in the history of Native Americans in Kentucky.

Take Exit 34 and continue southeast on KY 66. By now, you'll be deep inside the Daniel Boone National Forest. At the juncture of Upper Jack's Creek and Red Bird River, you'll soon come upon Red Bird Mission School with its grades K-12. Less than one mile farther, you'll see Red Bird Mission's Queendale Center at Beverly. (From the south take KY 66 north from Pineville.)

Drive in.

Cross over the bridge.

You'll see medical and dental clinics, pharmacy, early childhood development center, bookmobile, dormitories, cafeteria, food pantry, community store, and craft shop.

Divisions of Red Bird Mission include Education, Health and Wellness, Community Outreach, and Community Housing Improvement. The wellspring is volunteerism, the structure is shared religious belief, and the outcome is fulfilled hope in extending helping hands. The Mission thrives as an institution in the Red Bird Missionary Conference, which is associated with the General Board of Global Ministries of The United Methodist Church.

Community Outreach includes Elderly/Low Income Housing, Women and Children Ministries, and Christmas Assistance—three hundred and fifty children had a more joyous Christmas last year because there were ample people who cared enough to make it happen.

In the old Beverly Church on Cow Fork, original site of Red Bird Mission, essential words are written beside the pulpit—the biblical "Fruits of the Spirit:"

Love

Joy

Patience

Kindness

Goodwill

Faithfulness

Gentleness

Self-Control

As we sit in our rocking chairs here on Plum Lick, we tell ourselves, "Why don't we pick just one of those and spend some quality time with it?" Gentleness might garner goodwill. The payback of kindness could be joy. And above all, there might be an abundant measure of love.

Jane

You don't have to go it alone.

Sure, help has to begin *within* the individual, but there's a place and a person we'd like to tell you about. How fine it would be if her message were to reach someone you know—maybe, even yourself.

It may not seem like it right this minute, but it is possible to find the way out of abusive relationships. It's possible to discover a new self. There can be new opportunities. New ideas are waiting for the right person to come along. Yes, there is good news!

Jane Stephenson is a modern pioneering woman, Founder/Advisor of the New Opportunity School for Women. We recently sat with her in her Lexington home and talked about the fifteen-year-old project that has been the emotional and financial salvation of hundreds of Appalachian women.

"I think in growing up I came to realize that when you live in a rural area it is hard to find the help you need. My mission was to try to find these women on the verge of breaking out of situations. I tried to help rural women by providing resources to help with problems of life in a sensible and more productive way...a lot of women cannot leave farms and situations...we can take our workshops out to them."

New Opportunity School for Women, Inc., funded privately without federal or state money, is based on the campus of Berea

College. The mission: to improve the educational, financial, and personal circumstances of low-income, middle-aged women in Kentucky and the south central Appalachian region.

"An important component of (the project) is building self-esteem and confidence," says Kim Short, Director of Administration & Programs for New Opportunity School for Women, Inc. "Every effort is made to assure successes and a sense of accomplishments by participants in every aspect of the program. Each participant has received complete materials explaining their three-week stay in Berea. Once a participant has built her self-confidence, she can then see herself in a leadership role in her community and benefit by leadership development seminars, classes on public speaking, and learning about state and local government.

"A Career/Education Counselor provides services to local women and to expand our outreach mission into adjoining counties in the Appalachian region of Kentucky. The Counselor provides workshops and individual appointments to those women who cannot come to Berea for the three-week residential program. Services of the Counselor include skills and interest assessment, job search training, interview coaching, résumé and application development, basic skills training and tutoring, ACT preparation, time management, and leadership development."

Too good to be true?

Not at all.

"Three hundred and seventy-three women have completed the three-week residential program and an additional five hundred people are served each year through workshops in Berea and other locations in eastern Kentucky," says Kim. "From a recent survey of our graduates, seventy-six percent are employed, in school for further training, or both employed and in school. Of the graduates receiving public assistance prior to attending the New Opportunity School for Women, forty percent no longer do so, and additional thirty-two percent are enrolled in further education."

For anyone interested in participating in the New Opportunity School for Women, or if you know of someone who might benefit, here are the requirements for admission. "Twice a year fourteen women are selected to participate, at no cost to them, in a three-week residential education program on Berea College campus. In a lengthy application and interview process, the selection committee generally looks for strong motivation, financial need, and women who have participated in volunteer work within their own community. Selected participants must have a high school diploma, GED, or actively working on their GED. They must be between the ages of thirty to fifty-five, low income, from the Appalachian region, and agree to remain on campus for the entire three weeks, including weekends."

Jane Stephenson, Kim Short, and their associates are confident and sensitive women who care passionately about the commonwealth, where for too long a tradition has been to relegate women to the kitchen and the bedroom.

Jane wants "to try to help rural women by providing resource to help with problems of life in a sensible and more productive way." The idea is to help them with their families by being neither burdens to themselves nor their spouses and children. It means leadership and a betterment of deeply entrenched value systems.

Without federal or state funding, fundraising is ongoing. The Education foundation of America and a large base of individual donors and volunteers have helped to pave the way.

"What they are learning is being passed on," says Jane Stephenson, a woman with outstretched hand to women who have a need and are willing to break old patterns and move toward the future.

Louise

Her smile begins on the arch of her chin and moves up to her eyebrows.

Her entire face is a smile.

No frowns.

Louise Rogers Kimbrough was born in the Annville community of Jackson County. She was two months premature and weighed three pounds. Soon it would become apparent that something was visually abnormal.

"Mother sent me to New York, when I was not quite two years old, for surgery on my eyes. Until I was twenty-two I could read largest print and see colors. At twenty-two, I had a cornea transplant, but the retina detached and I lost total sight."

We're sitting with Louise in the lobby of the Kentucky Talking Book Library on the second floor of the Kentucky Archives in Frankfort. A conversation with this remarkable woman makes us want to get down on our knees and give thanks for being able to savor our daughter's auburn hair when it shines in the autumn sunlight. And we should remember to give more thanks for our daughter's ability to see us. We are among the lucky ones.

"I began reading Braille over sixty years ago (Louise is sixty-nine now), when I was in the first grade."

The occasion for our accidental meeting was the thirty-fifth anniversary of the Kentucky Talking Book Library (KTBL). Louise Kimbrough was there to enjoy the cake and to give testimony to the importance of the program that has almost five thousand patrons, ranging in age from two to one hundred and six.

Louise has never allowed blindness (she prefers that word to "visually challenged") to interfere with her joy for living and learning. She earned a master's degree in social work from Ohio State University, attended schools for the blind in Columbus, Ohio, and in Louisville, where she was a social worker. She moved to Chicago, where she was the editor of *Dialogue* magazine.

"Freelance writing is my favorite vocation. I still write a column 'Around the House,' recipes and hints (for the sight impaired). For example, when a recipe says 'cook until brown' (in a regular cookbook), how is a sightless person going to know when it's brown? By the way it feels or smells, of course!

"I've moonlighted all my life," said Louise, the smile broadening, the warmth of her good nature reaching toward us and beyond.

"I've proofed Braille since I was fourteen years old. Now I proof Braille by computer. They scan material into the computer, and I put in the commands to translate to Braille, read it, correct it, and send it back to the library."

There are eighty-nine volunteers who have recorded and monitored over 1,400 books at KTBL. There are 53,842 titles in KTBL's collection with approximately 500 books checked out each day—Braille books and books on tape as well as cassette players to play them—all free of charge and mailed postage paid to and from patrons.

Louise, who once met Helen Keller and was inspired by her, understood the need described by State Librarian Jim Nelson. "For those of us who browse the catalog and stacks of our local library, or the bustling isles of our local bookstore, it's difficult to understand a world where that is not possible. But for those who have lost their vision, this is a daily reality. Our staff not only helps our Talking Book patrons find reading materials to meet their interests, but they coordinate our amazing volunteers who record for them, as well as making sure these materials get to them in a timely manner."

As we sit with Louise, watch the smile moving with such naturalness, and listen to the clarity of her voice, we tell ourselves that it's time to tell her story to children and parents all around Kentucky.

As Louise sums it up "Blindness is not darkness, and it is not colorless.

"It's more like looking at water in a river at night. To be blind is perfectly respectable. It is not respectable to not do anything about it."

Lil

You couldn't pry her out of Kentucky if you tried. She's Boston-bred.

But her love is right here.

Lillian (just about everybody calls her "Lil")—Lucille Henken Press—is the wife of O. Leonard Press, founder of KET—Kentucky Educational Television—the largest Public Broadcasting member network in America.

Her role in the formation of KET?

"Patience," she says with a wry grin, "I did my own thing."

Graduating magna cum laude from Boston University with a B.S. in journalism, for four years she worked her way through college as a part-time newspaper reporter.

"I took night courses to graduate.

"I got an A+ in Contemporary Problems but I couldn't pass typing," she says with a laugh. "I was not cut out for that."

Lil says she naturally loves to study and it was on one of her college library trips that she connected with her helpmeet of over fifty years.

"Len asked me to lunch and we never dated anyone else." They married and went on to complete their masters degrees from Boston University.

Len brought his young bride with him when he came to Lexington to be program director at WBKY-FM (now WUKY-FM) and instructor at the University of Kentucky.

"I went to work for WVLK-AM (radio) the week that [the station] moved into the Phoenix Hotel." She started out writing commercials and quickly became program director.

Lil's vita reads like a happy marriage contract of volunteerism and cooperative effort. Words like "organized," "promoted," "created," "directed," "advised," "provided," and, yes, even "shepherded," are sprinkled throughout this transplanted Bostonian's vita, which spans years of caring deeply for the people of the Commonwealth of Kentucky.

After thirteen years of marriage, and moves back and forth from Kentucky to Washington D.C., Len and Lil produced a son, Lowell. "I didn't want to go to work any more. I stayed home for four or five years. After that is when I emerged."

Emerged and never looked back.

"I started out in 1962 going to nine counties as a volunteer with the Kentucky Department of Mental Health. They did cover my gasoline, but I had to hire a babysitter.

"I was a consultant on the payroll, in 1965. Two years later, Lowell went to the first grade and I joined the staff of the Kentucky Department of Mental Health as executive assistant to the commissioner until 1975."

During this time, she organized, promoted, and developed the first comprehensive community mental health boards and centers in Kentucky. The multi-county centers and boards served as a prototype for Kentucky's system, which came to be called "the best in the nation."

"For years, I had a sign over my desk that stated 'Patient welfare comes first.' It's fairly easy to come to a solution if all parties believe that," says Lil.

She went to Washington in 1980 as special assistant to the Federal co-chair to the Appalachian Commission. "I had an apartment there but came home to Kentucky every other week. I was there for three years."

Around 1982, there was a growing belief that Kentucky needed an honors academy for high school students. The idea was sold to then Gov. John Y. Brown and in 1983, the Kentucky Governor's Scholars Program was born—a five-week, residential summer program for outstanding Kentucky students.

Lil Press served as its director until 1993, but the school thrives to this day.

She didn't stop or limit herself: "I incorporated my idea for a national conference of Governor's Scholars schools." She led the way and became its first national president.

Since that time, she's found time to serve on the Board of Trustees at Centre College, where, she says, "I have found Centre to be an absolutely magical place. They have extremely high standards—they don't inflate grades—and people matter."

Thankfully, Lil's passion for humanity does not go unnoticed and, in 2004, she was awarded the Governor Martha Layne Collins Leadership Award by Women Leading Kentucky.

Lillian Lucille Henken Press doesn't show signs of slowing down, either. "My latest project is the Women's Network. We now have Advocates for Democratic Principles and that's mushrooming!" she says excitedly.

What do you say to young people (from other states) considering Kentucky as a place to live a meaningful life?

"If you come here with an open heart, with a genuine acceptance of the people and the place, there is nothing you cannot accomplish.

"There are wonderful people in Kentucky who will reach out and help you sell your ideas if they believe that is a way to uplift their communities or the young people of Kentucky.

"I think the biggest thing we need is passion. Cynicism won't get us there in these troubled times. "

An afternoon with Lillian Press is like a visit to a sawmill running full tilt where timber comes in raw, but goes out in a variety of creations ready for carpenters with hammers and nails.

Jackie

"Good morning!"

"How are you?"

"I'm fine. How are you?"

"Fine. Hope you have a good day."

"You too."

"You" and "good" were two of Postmaster Jackie Lush's favorite words. When she sang them out it was with a sincere and cheerful tone, the kind sorely needed in this time of national and international tension.

No matter what's happening in the national capitals of the world, it's normally another quiet day at North Middletown, Kentucky 40357. Another box holder has come and gone from the tiny post office on Main Street. Little and sometimes major aches and pains have been shared, weather discussed—politics and religion seldom mentioned.

It's an oasis is what it is, and it measures only about three hundred and eighty square feet, counting the counter, lobby, mailbox wall and the work area behind it. It's about the size of a kitchen or a one-car garage. There's no parking lot, no loading dock—just one small door and a couple of windows.

Jackie Lush, the postmaster, came to the one and only service window as needed where she sold stamps, wrote money orders, insured and weighed packages. She did it all without the benefit of a computer the way they do it fancy in the big city. Here in North Middletown—population about six hundred—there's usually not a line of patrons. It's a little farming community located in Bourbon County, not to be confused with Middletown in Jefferson County. (North Middletown is south of Middletown.)

Jackie said she didn't want to be any place any bigger or more technologically advanced. "Sixty percent of all post offices in the U.S. are in small communities and I love being here. People are very understanding. It's wonderful, a blessing. I want North Middletown to have a good level of service."

This smiling postmaster grew up as a farm girl and from those roots learned the values that have sustained her down through the years. "My grandfather was one hundred years old. He loved his mules and his fifty acres. Everything was very friendly, you knew people on a personal basis," said Jackie, who considered herself to be a "part of the family."

She provided a personal service to the people of North Middletown, "...a place where people can come in and talk and laugh." It's a connection that transcends the gas pump and the grocery counter.

"Sweetie, what can I get you?" sang Jackie to a customer who came in and cleared his throat.

"I seem to have misplaced my key," said the rueful renter of one of the fewer than two hundred boxes. (Jackie usually had the mail in the boxes by ten o'clock in the morning. The rest of the day was nonstop public service.)

Jackie cheerfully handed over the mail and reassured the keyless, "I'm sure you'll find it!"

After the door closed, Jackie mused: "I try to get people to use their key, some people never do." But she added, without regret: "I'm here for service for heaven's sake."

Jackie Lush was one of almost five hundred female postmasters in Kentucky. She's was there in the winter, when she strung her Christmas lights and stayed warm by a little gas heater. She was there in the springtime, when boxes of baby chicks added to the usual chatter of farm family members looking forward to a new season of encouragement. She was there in the summertime, when the little three hundred and eighty-square-foot oasis was cooled by a small air purifier and air conditioner on the wall. She was there in the autumn, when leaves began to turn and gather on the sidewalk, where the postmaster tended her flowers as carefully as her customers.

Jackie carefully planned her retirement and now she's gone and done it. What will she do after twenty-six years of postal work, eleven years at the North Middletown post office, thirty-four years as a government employee?

"I want to do a lot of things I've not had time to do," she said as she lowered the service window at the end of the last day. She no longer has to make the forty-mile roundtrip from her home in Winchester, doesn't have to spring into action when somebody has misplaced a postal box key, doesn't have to fill out "reports, reports...always something...cleaning out the fiscal year files." Doesn't have to worry about the garbage can outside or her voluntary newspaper recycling bin inside. Doesn't have to pick up the cans thrown into the bushes.

A tradition of female postmasters has flourished in North Middletown, although from time to time there's been a man in charge. By the way, does Jackie want to be called post*mistress* the way so many insist on chair*woman* or chair*person* or just plain *chair*? She has ruled out post*woman*, post*person*, and certainly just plain *post*. Jackie Lush was proud to be the post*master* of North Middletown, Kentucky 40357.

The new postmaster is Sheila Hawkins. Send her a card and wish her good luck!

Paula

This Kentucky lady doesn't have time to weep. She's too busy stirring the pots.

Paula Cunningham's passion is producing first-rate products for young and old—it doesn't matter whether the stove is in the farmhouse or the townhouse. Paula is most at home in her own house—McClanahan Publishing House—where enticing recipes abound, along with some new formulas for book publishing.

"In the early 80s, I was pregnant with our twins (two of their five sons)," says Paula, "when my husband, Bill, asked me to find a publisher for his book, *Flames in the Wind*. I found a company in Tennessee and they published it, but Bill and I did all the work! The next one, *On Bended Knees* (about the Kentucky and Tennessee tobacco wars) we published ourselves. It was published in November and we sold out of the press run of two thousand books by December."

With this taste of success under her apron and armed with her degree in merchandising from Winthrop University in South Carolina, Paula edited *Sample West Kentucky*, a collection of recipes from Western Kentucky restaurants. She subsequently joined nationally acclaimed chef Curtis Grace in the kitchen and, discovering a need, wasted no time in meeting a hearty appetite for really good cookbooks.

Paula knew, all across Kentucky, from the mouth of the Cumberland River at Smithland to Poor Fork in Letcher County, there's a craving for the best the kitchen can provide.

Located in Kuttawa in Lyon County on the banks of the Cumberland River, Paula's warehouse shelves are lined with cookbooks from the fanciest, such as Mr. Grace's *Encore*, to one of our favorites, *Kentucky Keepsakes*, by Elizabeth Ross. By the way, in 1997, that one sold 2,500 copies on QVC, the television shopping network, in just five minutes!

Since 1983, her publishing firm has published over ninety titles. About seventy percent are cookbooks, the rest range from historical to contemporary, including husband Bill's *Castle*, to a recently published book by Patti Starr, *Ghost Hunting in Kentucky and Beyond*, which might also appeal to those who haunt the pantry.

Speaking of hearty appetites, as a soccer mom who helped raise five boys during formative years, one book Paula produced was *The Soccer Mom Cookbook*, a collection of simple dishes for families on the go. That one, along with many others, is still in print and available through her website *www.kybooks.com*.

Paula and her staff of two full-time employees, Michelle Stone (who has also authored three of McClanahan's *Merry Christmas from ---- cookbooks*), Jo Doty and Gordon Sims, part-time warehouse manager, are the only ingredients in this successful stew. They take their show on the road all over the United States whenever they can to show what a Kentucky businesswoman can serve up. They've even had a book signing at Neiman Marcus in Texas. Now, that's no small tidbit!

Here's another idea Paula is cooking up. "So far, it's responsible for a twenty percent increase in our revenues," says Paula.

"There are so many people who have a good idea for a book and have the money to produce it, but don't know how," she says. This is where her newest marketing strategy comes in.

"This is not vanity press. The best title I can come up with is 'Book Packaging.' We help them with designing the cover and the book's layout, typesetting, and getting the proper registration numbers so that their books may be sold at any bookstore in the country. We basically hold their hand through the book publishing process."

If this piques your interest, just remember the last and most important ingredient in this venture is *you*. That means, when the books arrive, the truck pulls up to your garage and it's up to you to take it from there. Production is the easy, fun part—now comes the real work!

"We can go even further with our Book Packaging program in that we also help them produce press releases and instruct them on how to sell to special outlets such as libraries. We do everything but distribute and sell the books."

Two of her recent "book packagings" have been a history of the University of Kentucky's medical school and a cookbook written by members of the Garden Club of Kentucky.

"It has just been amazing," says Paula. "We haven't sought out anyone to help, they just find us."

Any advice for would-be authors?

"Don't be discouraged," Paula says. "You've got to have lots of tough skin, but you've got to submit, submit, submit (to publishers) to find out what the publishers are looking for."

Any advice for would-be publishers?

"Find your niche, do what you do best and stick with it. We cannot compete with the big New York publishers, but in Kentucky we're doing what is best for us," Paula says emphatically.

Bill

"Until you go to Kentucky and with your own eyes behold the Derby, you ain't never been nowheres and you ain't never seen nothin'!" Kentucky author Irvin S. Cobb once said.

Whoa back!

Wait a minute, Hoss!

Folks are apt to think Kentuckians tawk funny on a regular basis, and don't become fully bright until the first Saturday in May.

You could just as easily say, "Until you go to a thoroughbred farm in Kentucky and with your own eyes behold the sun coming up as winter converges into spring, you haven't been too many places and haven't seen the likes of what we have around these Bluegrass parts."

When the sun breaks through the layered clouds of pale blue and blended gold over the juncture of Donaldson and Stoner Creeks just over the ridges from Pretty Run Creek, a man goes to his stable day after day and turns out the mares from the maternity stalls.

Bill Dickson—seventh generation to live on this carpet of limestone- based soil, nurturing the bone density of those flying legs—mucks the stalls, counts the days leading to the breeding shed, dreams the dream of another Run for the Roses—the "greatest two minutes in sports."

Here's the thing.

The first Saturday in May is the glorious, flower-bedecked day at Churchill Downs in Louisville. Ladies sally 'round with their saucy hats and lads and lassies duel with elbows and beer containers in the infield, while the money-honeys sip mint juleps up there on Millionaire's Row.

Every day is Derby Day at Glen Oak Farm and hundreds of other thoroughbred farms in the inner Bluegrass.

There's more to it than beautiful clothes bleeding on television and bare skin sweating at the center of the mile and a quarter oval. There's something called work back home on the farm.

Bill Dickson boards horses for owners as far away as India, Australia, New Zealand, and Japan. He's responsible for twenty to thirty mares, making sure that their not-uncommon $100,000 stud-fee foals arrive as close as possible to New Years Day, universal birthday for all thoroughbreds.

With about five hundred gently rolling acres to fence and make safe for animals valued at hundreds of thousands of dollars, Bill also manages his cows and calves—the total herd is approximately one hundred—and every last one of them eats!

Bill produces about 20,000 square bales and eight hundred round bails of hay, principally alfalfa, which he markets to clients in the area.

There was a time when such a farm might involve many workers living in tenant houses, but now machinery and carefully constructed facilities make what amounts to a one-man operation not only a possibility but a necessity. One full-time employee lends a helping hand, but the key words are *businesslike* and *down-to-earth*.

This rolling earth—populated with two- and three-hundred-year-old burr oak and ash and younger sycamores, is a Camelot requiring constant attention and boundless energy—a family tradition. Bill's pioneer ancestor John Rice built the white-column home in 1810 and some of his children are buried nearby, graves marked with simplicity and respect.

The passing generations have witnessed the incomparable view from atop the highest hill, and when the sun goes down there's a spreading view of the land that constitutes the infrastructure for such magical moments as Monday, May 17, 1875—the first running of the Kentucky Derby.

The first of the Derby winners was Aristides, ridden by Oliver Lewis, an African-American. You may read about it in Jim Bolus's book, *Run for the Roses: 100 years at the Kentucky Derby*, which was published, in 1974. Bolus and Joe Hirsch co-authored *Kentucky Derby: The Chance of a Lifetime*, in 1988.

When future first Saturdays in May come thundering down the homestretch, Bill Dickson and his family at Glen Oak Farm may be standing at the winner's circle. But—

"Just to own a mare and breed a Kentucky Derby winner" is victory enough, says Bill, who has about fifty years more to make it happen.

Until then, it takes infinite patience and a calm state of mind if there's to be a length of a chance in this "Sport of Kings."

At foaling time, Bill sleeps in one-hour stretches. There's a short, determined walk from the house to the stable and back again from the stable to the house, as many as it takes. Sometimes, the path is over a late winter snow with big and shiny Kentucky quarter-sized flakes floating down from a heavy, blowing, pregnant sky.

"Hello, Ladies," says Bill as he checks each stall—one foal and four to go, the mares answering with doleful looks, head shakes, and gnaws on wooden beams.

"Don't eat my barn," says Bill, knowing that you don't what-for a thoroughbred when she's about to foal. He walks back to the house and tastes the snow on the tip of his tongue.

That's Bill's wreath of roses.

Candy Making

Without Mary's mother, there would be no candy tradition. She passed away when Mary was four years old. All Mary has now is a tattered and yellowing composition book filled with Mother's candy recipes.

Elizabeth Anderson, the first generation, made candy in the 1920s and developed recipes for almost all the candy that her descendants produce today.

Mary Mark, Rooney Gray, and Francie Prier, the second and third generations, and friend Sue Newkirk, make pounds and pounds of delicious candies and give it away. But, they guard the recipes. Friends and family will just have to go on expecting rich morsels as part of their own Christmas rituals.

The second and third generations begin on a late Thursday morning and by Saturday the three, fourth-generation girls Catherine, Mary Elizabeth, and Abby arrive from college.

Sometimes they have friends in tow who'll usually wind up washing dishes—and loving it.

The kitchen is one hundred and fifty square feet. Back porch doors are left wide open to cool things off inside.

The ladies fiddle with a new-fangled digital thermometer, one with a probe and a small hand-held digital reader, but the old tried-and-true glass tube was holding forth in the bubbling pot of cream and sugar.

"Don't touch that 'til it's at least at two hundred and fifty-two," says Francie, squinting at the small lines on the thermometer.

"You just can't make candy on a humid day," says Rooney. "You need cold, dry air. Candy is fickle."

Other than the new stove in the kitchen, there isn't any special equipment. "We have pans designated as 'the candy pot,' a few spoons, measuring cups," says Mary. "My first dipper for bonbons was a piece of bailing wire."

"Comin' through!" warns Rooney as she hefts from the stove the large pot filled with bubbling cream and sugar. It's at the scalding stage. She's heading for the back door and in one smooth motion, she pours the sweet concoction out onto the waiting cold, buttered marble.

Twelve kinds of candy, six to eight different flavors—at an average of one hundred and fifty pounds of sugar a year in fifty years of candy making, that's over 7,500 pounds of the sweet stuff!

"We've gone through about one hundred and twenty-five pounds of sugar already this weekend," says Sue. "Some years we have used as much as three hundred pounds."

Sugar's not all—cases of corn syrup, cases of whipping cream, pounds and pounds of butter, hard candy flavors, and endless pounds of chocolate.

And laughter.

Lots and lots of laughter!

"How far are you away from cutting, Momma?" asks Rooney.

"When I hit the hook, it was 10:25, so it's about ready to come off. If Mandy said twenty minutes," chuckles Mary. "You pull it for twenty minutes." Mandy was Mary's mother's candy-making helper.

"Here's a strip, y'all" Mary says as she slowly pulls the cream candy into a satiny ribbon using a gentle, but firm rhythm.

"How do you know if it's a 'good' making?"

"If it tastes good and looks nice, we'll package it," says Rooney.

"Over the years we've thrown away very, very little. We've scorched rocha, but we just broke it up and put it on ice cream."

Catherine discovers that cocoa-flavored rum might resurrect the coconut centers for bonbons, if it's cooked too dry.

"Takes almost as long as almond rocha to cook," says Rooney, "I could live without it, but John's family thinks it's the only thing we make."

Rooney is now taking orders for her own brand of candy in the Hodgenville area–MAM Candies–made to order and packaged in elegant foil boxes. Caramels are Rooney's specialty. Chocolate-dipped caramels, too. "My bourbon balls usually make you sit up and say 'Hell-0!'"

"Hey, y'all, this cream candy is crawling to longer-length pieces," says Sue bending over one of the brown slabs of marble decorated with cut pieces of white cream candy. "I'll cut if you'll straighten 'em out," she says to Lalie, the spare hand.

When the pulled candy is cut and resting on the marble, there will always be end pieces, the "uglies," that are either scooped up by Boardie, Mary's husband of fifty-seven years, or are fair game for sweet-toothed nibblers.

Francie says she can't pull cream candy, because she has "hot hands" and the candy "goes to worms." But she is outstanding with log cabin rolls. She and Sue are in the dining room working hard with smooth, constant motion to change the chewy candy into an almost powdery consistency.

Each of them has her own specialty. Mary's is rocha, Rooney's is cream candy and caramels, Francie is the hard candy queen and Sue keeps everybody laughing. "I just go wherever I'm needed," she giggles.

"If I didn't take home a piece of candy, I would still make the trip from Louisville just to be with these wonderful people."

Sweet.

Wee Books

My mother used to tell me to think big, but she said that there might be, just might be, a time and place for some really small things. Mothers have a way of knowing the importance of the smallest of creatures.

It goes with woman's intuition.

But, I had no idea I would ever run smack into anything as little as Joyce Barton's tiny, tiny, tiny books and her tiny, tiny, tiny Christmas House at Bluebird Acres in northwestern Knox County, just down the road from Woodbine.

Breathtaking.

Amazing.

Inspiring.

I pulled up a chair and with thumb and forefinger, gingerly took one of the miniature books and placed it lightly in the palm of my hand the way I'd place a postage stamp there, or maybe a quarter. The construction was a combination of intuition, patience, and nimble fingers.

Small.

Really small.

But the contents are really big. Like, in forty tiny pages, are all the recipes you'd need for an entire Thanksgiving dinner.

Really.

How about an illustration of the Cherokee alphabet? A book of presidents? The Lord's Prayer in seven different languages on pages five-by-five millimeters by three millimeters thick?

We're talking about much more than the world's smallest books. Joyce Barton is obsessed with miniaturization—if it's small, how can it be smaller and still tell a story? She even has a tiny library full of books she has made by hand.

There's also the outbuilding housing the Christmas House depicting everyday Bethlehem scenes—women washing clothes at the river... workers stomping grapes beneath the palm trees. The Holy Land without buying the airline ticket. The Mount of Olives without all the noise, or pushing and shoving.

And, there's Santa Land: "Looks as if Mrs. Claus has been in there—see the biscuits on the kitchen table...the pieced quilts in the bedroom?" asks miniaturist Joyce Barton, beaming with a larger-than-life pride of unusual accomplishment. Her hands are her jeweler's tools, but her heart is as big as tomorrow.

There're the candy factory assembly line, the Reindeer Flight School (Comet and Donner have to know the instrumentation), up, up, and away high over the Eskimo Village with the ice fishing and the Polar bears watching, the dog teams straining. Everywhere you look there's something to marvel about, enough to make grown folks long for childhood days of yore.

Joyce Barton has been collecting and creating miniatures of all types for thirty to thirty-five years. She and her seventy-one-year-old husband don't throw anything away: the tiny white peacock her grandmother gave her—"no use for it, but just liked it." She put it as a guardian at the entrance of the main crèche in Bethlehem.

There's a twinkling, star-studded night sky over the wee skating rink with a model train circling—"used to have it snowing in here, but the mechanism is down." Sleighs and horses with tiny bells and flowing scarves...the Main Street Bakery...a church complete with organ and pews ...a coal mine and tipple...replicas of buildings where Joyce and Carl went to school.

After all, she was the school librarian, then the regional librarian. So, why not retire to become the chief executive officer of Bluebird Press where everything is a little work in progress?

"In the springtime, there's so much to do," say Joyce and Carl Barton, their old farm house surrounded by buggy wheels, wagon wheels, and horse collars—a likely place for school children to visit, and they do, by the hundreds.

Visitors are fascinated by the goldfish in the three hundred-gallon fishpond with blooming lilies and a banana tree.

"All we do is piddle 'round," says Joyce as we stroll past the birdhouse gourds, "My father's rock collection," the rock-slab table with the dinosaur bone embedded, a fifty-two-inch Noah's Ark with all the animals, two by two.

"We don't count money any more," says Mrs. Noah as Mr. Noah nods approval. She likes to trade and make a few wholesale deals with interested parties all across the country.

Yes, Virginia, there is a small market for small things. It begins with a small idea and a big imagination.

As I sit down for a generous slice of homemade pie and a cup of coffee, several things come to mind, and I'm grateful to be able to take them home with me.

The biggest things are actually the smallest—such as the smiles at Bluebird Press, quiet agreements that everybody has a story to tell, especially the short, short, short story.

Next time you think there's nothing big enough to matter, take a little trip to the Bluebird kingdom and get lost in imagination. Your reward will be bigger than life itself.

Cheryl

Twenty-three-year-old Tracy Kenney had been searching the bookmobile shelves for her usual six- to eight-book checkout, and she was looking for more.

"She's my best reader in North Middletown," the Asparagus Lady said to a grinning Tracy as she exited with her bag of books.

Cheryl Stone, known in Bourbon County as "The Asparagus Lady," has become "The Bookmobile Lady" to readers ranging in age from pre-kindergarten to a ninety-two-year old patron with a penchant for romance novels.

"When I go to see her, I take more than just books," smiles Cheryl. "She wants you to sit in that rocking chair for five to ten minutes, have an orange pop and tell her what's going on the farm."

What's going on down on the farm is the reason Cheryl has pursued another career.

"We put in sixteen-hour days on the farm, I'm not getting any younger, and I needed the money," says Cheryl, matter of factly.

"Robert and I grow an acre of asparagus and it is backbreaking work walking down those long rows. It's picked by hand everyday—fifty to seventy pounds, some days. One customer we have wants thirty to one hundred pounds twice a week to take to the Farmer's Market."

Asparagus isn't the only thing grown, marketed, and distributed from Stone Home Farm's two hundred acres. There's the corn that's shelled out and sold in fifty-pound sacks to a local farm supply store, the fields of rye straw, alfalfa, soybeans, and a 15,000-pound tobacco base to be worked, harvested, and sold—along with the fruit of forty bushes of blueberries.

"We have to fight the birds for the blueberries," says Asparagus Lady with a shake of her head, "And they will attack if you get close enough. We've tried everything we can think of—fake bird distress calls (that worked about ten minutes) tobacco cottons over the bushes (the birds get in under the cottons), and Robert gets out there with a shotgun, but even that doesn't chase them off for too long.

"We tried U-pick strawberries, but too many people wanted me to pick them," laughs Cheryl, "And we were picking strawberries all day! Two years ago we stopped doing farmers markets and street sales three times a week, but I still make house-to-house deliveries on my lunch hour and after work."

Cheryl has customers who order asparagus a pound or two at a time and when she's not on her bookmobile route, she's delivering asparagus or blueberries to homes, or the courthouse, or the bank, or the library.

Robert, Cheryl's talented Cornell University-Agribusiness-educated husband still works sunup until after sundown. "Sometimes he's not stopped to eat anything until after ten o'clock at night," she says.

In addition to farming with Robert, Cheryl has been working October through March at a local tobacco warehouse and part-time at a local bank. A couple of years ago, the Bourbon County Conservation District awarded them the coveted Master Conservationist distinction.

"We don't have cattle because we have no good fences. We took out all the interior fencing to raise the crops." Cheryl Rolls her eyes as she recounts the story of how the day before company was to arrive, a neighbor's fifty head of cattle visited her yard.

"Those cows ate all the impatiens and left cowpiles all over the front yard!"

Asparagus Lady grew up on a farm in Oregon, where her grandfather had farmed, and that's where she formed her love for being out of doors. "My dad lived on the land but didn't farm it. After high school I wanted to go into law enforcement and wound up in Washington DC with the FBI fingerprinting office."

To make several years short, Cheryl came to Kentucky and met Robert at the church where they now attend at the little crossroads of Clintonville.

They've hired someone to help do the heavy farming with Robert, but Cheryl still helps out with lighter duties—mowing, filling orders, etc. After Cheryl's doctor told her that she couldn't keep on slinging around fifty-pound bales of hay, she knew that she was going to have to find full-time work elsewhere. "Robert even tried to make lighter, forty-pound bales for me," says Cheryl.

"I didn't want to hate the farm. As a matter of fact, I would love it if we could buy a smaller farm with road frontage so we could market our produce right there. Robert's a good gardener and he could raise the best sweet corn and raspberries. We do raise wonderful raspberries.

"Robert knew that I was looking for a full-time job, and he wanted me to find something that I really wanted to do. I didn't want to be sitting behind a desk. I wanted to be outside."

So now, Cheryl Stone is delivering more than asparagus and blueberries, she's delivering books to children and shut-ins.

"Sometimes I just sit and read to the kids in the bookmobile, and they love it.

"I love it."

Inez

Inez is tucked away deep in the Appalachian Mountains of eastern Kentucky. It's a tiny Martin County town, but it reaches up toward taller expectations. A central gleam of this diamond in the highlands is a committed sense of place and state of mind.

It's a dream come true for a regional son like Mike Duncan, another of those community leaders deeply proud of his Appalachian heritage. They've not surrendered to Hollywood's stereotype that in order for Kentuckians to be marketable entertainment, they must be sinking in homegrown depravity.

Twenty years ago, Mr. Duncan, a native of Oneida in Clay County, graduate of Cumberland College in Whitley County, banker in Lawrence and Martin counties, was living proof of one of our main Plum Lick beliefs: "You can go home again, and probably should!"

"Mike" Duncan, CEO and chairman of the board of Inez Deposit Bank and First National Bank of Louisa, in adjoining Lawrence County, is the founder of the "Summer Internship Program," nationally recognized as far away as New York and California.

Los Angeles Times journalist Judy Pasternak has written of Mike Duncan's internship program: "The banker offers challenging work, individual counseling, career contacts, seminars, and outings for as many years as each student needs, through high school, college, and beyond. In return, he asks "the pledge," summed up in the notes he scribbles for his yearly welcome speech:

"Give something back. Return the favor. Get involved. Help find your way back home."

Each spring, Mike Duncan invites the top ten percent of the junior class at Lawrence County High School and the top twenty-five percent of the junior class from Sheldon Clark High School, in Martin County, to apply for the Summer Intern Program at his bank in Inez.

This particular year, there were eleven energized eastern Kentucky youths seated around the conference table in a room lined with books. Subjects included government, history, and literature.

Each intern had a large notebook filled with ideas about democracy, majority rule and minority rights, informed citizenry, decision making, and individual liberties.

Each of Mike Duncan's interns is expected to be familiar with Kentucky's Appalachian Development Plan of which native Lawrence Countian, former Governor Paul Patton has written in the foreword: "Because Appalachian Kentucky is not a region alone in the commonwealth, our Appalachian development strategy has been re-engineered to mesh with the development strategy for the entire state. Kentucky cannot advance if any region lags behind; Appalachian Kentucky cannot move ahead without a program that compliments goals for the state as a whole."

The interns assembled each year by Mike Duncan will move far beyond what most can imagine. They'll come to a better understanding of declining coal and tobacco production, all the more crucial when population growth percentages are factored in.

These are bipartisan realities (Gov. Patton is a Democrat, Mike Duncan is a Republican) and resolution lies somewhere in the middle—it arises from determined individual endeavors with the good of the community as a higher goal:

- Quality education
- Strong work ethic
- Improved moral character
- Pride in sense of place
- Unselfish paybacks

An invited speaker at this year's internship program in Inez, was encouraged by what he saw and heard, and it made the view from Plum Lick seem more promising without cause for hand wringing. It was high time for applause.

Mike Angel

When Mike Angel gets to Heaven he'll likely be making chairs. Chairs are his passion. Chairs are his persuasion. Chairs are his getting up and his sitting down.

A visit to Mike's Red Dog Mule-Ear Chair workshop in Laurel County is a trip back into time when people got down from their high horses and enjoyed the feeling of back and arms, legs and rear end nestled comfortably in the embrace of mock orange.

Maybe black walnut.

Or hickory.

Mike's a former U.S. Marine, marathon runner, Kentucky State Trooper, retired Alcohol, Tobacco, and Firearms Agent, and survivor of a drug raid gone wrong six years ago in Cleveland, Ohio. He's got two metal plates holding his right leg together leaving him with the gift of a barely noticeable limp. He's a survivor of a heart attack last fall (in, of all places, Deadwood, South Dakota), which has put him on a doctor-ordered strict diet in order to lose weight. Surely, Mike's guardian angel lives somewhere in the wood shavings of another Kentucky Mule-Ear Chair.

More likely it's "Fredi," Mike's wife, retired executive secretary, who helps in the painstaking finishing process as each chair moves from rawest stave to smoothest outcome. Behind every good chair maker there's an angel hard at work? Being married to a consummate chair maker may not be the easiest of callings. Or, it could be, as Fredi says, relaxing. It all comes down to individuality.

Angel Acres Road climbs a curving trail graced with recently planted trees—a log house at the top and a chair maker's shop to the side.

"Mike, are you here?"

"David?" asks Mike Angel, expecting the visit. He gingerly climbs the steps from the lower shop to the show room, smile on his face, firm hand outstretched. Fredi is away doing errands, so Mike and David sit in hickory rocking chairs and talk about one of Kentucky's vanishing arts.

"Hickory bark's up in springtime and early summer. Shave off the outside bark to get to the cambium layer (secondary wood tissues most suitable for chair making)."

Mike is patient with his visitor who wouldn't know a mock orange from mock turtle soup. Chair-making simplicity combined with exacting craftsmanship results in pleasure for the harried human condition.

David lets his fingers find their comfort zones in the curved arm ends of the "Mule-Ear," feel the support of the gentle staves against aging sacroiliac, allow the cerebellum to rest nicely and untroubled in the reassuring world of hickory.

"Fishing's too slow, golf's not productive," says Mike. "I built this building from scratch—1,800 square feet below, 1,800 square feet above—built on a shoestring." The shop today is filled with lots of "shoestrings"—another way of saying a one-hundred-year-old wood worker's press, a homemade "sauna bath" to make pieces of wood more bendable, and hand tools galore.

When he "retired" six years ago, he decided he wanted to spend the rest of his life surrounded by family—mother, father, sister, and brother. Mike was able to share the last two years of his father's life and that was another gift. Mike and Fredi's son, who'll retire from

ATF in about fourteen years, will also come back to continue his parents' love affair with chairs.

How many "Mule-Ears" have been made here so far? In the thousands, says Mike, who has customers far beyond Laurel County. He says he's so busy in his "retirement" he can't do it all. So he sends chairs to a man in Jackson County to weave the bottoms. Another man sends mesquite wood from Texas and a local bluegrass musician drops by to check on a recently installed furnace. A friend from New York comes in to borrow a pickup truck.

Says he's coming back to Kentucky, too—one day.

Kentucky Crafted

If you've a whimsy to treat your family and yourself to a heartwarming get-together, here's an idea to strap on for size. There's possibly no greater collective pleasure (and bargain) than the annual Kentucky Crafted: The Market.

It's held at the Kentucky Fair and Exposition Center in Louisville. The dates are usually around March 1, and it's open to the public from 9 a.m. until 6 p.m. on Saturday and noon to 5 p.m. on Sunday. Tickets are reasonable for adults and children, but a child under six years of age is admitted free—the time in our lives when we're most favorable for learning.

Imagine the impressions a child will take home from a wonderland of arts and crafts: wooden trains and horses, bird houses, Santa Claus collectibles. Older folks will marvel at delicate glass ornaments, colorful woolen rugs, exquisite furniture and jewelry—all truly handmade in Kentucky, not what falls off the end of a long, impersonal, robotized assembly line.

The dividing line between a child and a grownup has the rich possibility of being hardly recognizable, so adults will be forgiven for unabashed enthusiasm for the hand-crafted work of more than two hundred and seventy-five exhibitors from the Big Sandy to the Mississippi.

Each year, many authors from the Kentucky Book Fair are on hand with books about Kentucky, past and present. Writing has taken a proper place among the craftsmanship of traditional artisans. There are signings of first editions, a wide variety of cultural pleasures—gifts and keepsakes for every fancy—and tailor-made educational exhibitions just for children.

Children and grownups have a unique opportunity to see Kentucky and Kentuckians being their best and truest selves, not their cinematic, stereotypical, soap opera and cartoon silliest. We allow ourselves to become Beverly Hillbillies when we allow others to define ourselves even though we know better. Usually, it's done in order to create blockbusters of vaudeville, violence, and value standing on its head. The way to perpetuate it is to think its funny, pay the piper, and not stop laughing.

A day at the Kentucky Crafted: The Market can and probably will be memorable. Colors: everywhere. Sights: as refreshing as the seasons of centuries past and just begun. Sounds: pleasant and ripe for the taking. Conversations: imagine the possibilities.

"What better way to celebrate the Millennium than to bring back many of the wonderful craftspeople that have been part of The Market's success and history for nearly twenty years," says Program Director Fran Redmon.

Recently, when we gave a Kentucky Humanities Council talk at the Anderson County Middle School, we noticed a sign in the hallway: "Learning is a participatory activity." That's one of the best thoughts about Kentucky Crafted. It's one thing to go to The Market to look and listen and chatter. It's a better thing to desire to return

143

home to pick up the crafting tool, to want to take raw material and fashion it into an individual creation—actually to achieve an upland of originality.

Kentucky is alive and well. It has its problems, just as Hollywood and New York City have theirs. But, there is more than one Kentucky Cycle. Even though Kentucky Crafted won't win a Pulitzer, it stands a very good chance of helping to break the cynical round of negative thinking about mountains and hollows that have been stereotyped until they're almost unrecognizable.

Little by little, these perceptions are changing. Recently, a lady told us of her decision to leave Connecticut and to move to Breckinridge County, Kentucky. Another told of moving from Pennsylvania to Harrison County. A couple from Chicago was in Boyle and Casey counties—said they were looking for a new home away from the third largest city in the United States.

One of the many happenings that's making a positive difference is Kentucky Crafted: The Market.

See you there!

Freddie

Freddie Bevins would like to have a special Christmas present.

It's not the sort of thing that can be bought from a show room or a gift catalog—not a car, a boat, nor a skateboard.

Freddie wants a bone marrow transplant.

He's a teenager with a lifelong medical condition called hypergammaglobinanemia and severe chronic neutropenia, which means his immune system doesn't work the way it should. He could scratch his finger and it could be life threatening.

"I'm hoping someone out there will know of someone who can find it in their heart to help us," says Freddie's mother, Shirley.

When sufficient funds are raised, the bone transplant will probably be done at Duke University, which means Shirley will have to move to Durham, North Carolina, for the approximately two years required for the completion of the procedure, which could save Freddie's life. A more recent option is in Louisville.

"God has seen that he lives way past the time that the doctors gave him as a baby. He's a good teenager but has been through eighteen years of hospitals and surgeries."

Contributions may be made to The Bevins Transplant Fund, c/o The Citizens Deposit Bank and Trust Company located in Vanceburg (Lewis County).

The money will be held in trust until the time of the transplant.

Freddie has been living a life similar to "David The Bubble Boy," one of the last stories I covered as a CBS News correspondent. My heart went out to David, and I felt his pain all the more because our given names were the same. At that time I was not allowed to make a direct appeal for help. It's called objective reporting. I was in Houston when David died because his bone marrow transplant was unsuccessful.

Now there's Freddie.

He and I are headed down a bumpy road.

My elevated PSA (prostate-specific antigen) is real but it's nothing compared to Freddie's immune system deficiency, and this time around I can speak out, and I can say to Freddie's mother, help will be on the way.

May not be perfect, may not be all she and her family need to cope with the huge medical bills, but little by little, piece by piece, a resolution will occur. Each coin in the bone-transplant jars on the street- and-roadside shelves of giving is important and appreciated.

Out of respect for Freddie's precarious situation, I decided not to drive over to Lewis County to visit with him face to face, because even a sniffle from me could be his undoing. And I could never live with that. But, we'll communicate!

Here's a young man who never asked to be one of the only twenty-three people worldwide who are believed to have this rare condition called hypergammaglobinanemia and severe chronic neutropenia. He didn't ask to be barred from the basketball floor or the football field. He would have liked to have spent irreplaceable years with his peers. Schooled at home, he just knuckled down and made the most of the hand he was dealt.

Freddie Bevins is a fighter. His mother, Shirley, and his father, Fred, are a family who have looked for answers beyond all the IVs and morphine injections as many of the rest of us have looked beyond radiation and hormonal therapy to counter other unfriendly cells that have invaded our bodies.

Our families, sharing in common cause, are reminded that what we all should do is to pray for health, pray for recovery when we're not well, and dedicate our lives to reducing human suffering whenever and where ever we can.

It just means living one day at a time, enjoying and being grateful for the essence of one more holiday season and the passing of another year on Mother Earth, where there's always room for optimism!

The best is yet to come.

Michael

Michael Comer is a seventeen-year-old farm boy from Indiana. For the past fourteen years, he's been coming to Shriners Hospital for Children in Lexington, Kentucky.

When he was three years old, Michael and his older brother were playing follow the leader behind their grandfather's riding mower.

Michael was run over.

"I lost half of my knee and three of my toes," says Michael, who can't remember the actual day when the accident happened.

"About ten years ago I used to have all kinds of nightmares until I got some therapy."

Michael got more than therapy. Thanks to the Shriners Hospital for Children ("crippled" is no longer a part of the name)—he received a new kind of left leg and knee. The accident "cut half the growth plates out of my knee, which made my leg grow crooked. So they killed the rest of the growth plates in my knee, so my leg doesn't grow as fast. About every five years or so they have to go in and lengthen my leg to make it catch up with my good one."

Three times, after "growth spurts," surgeons at Shriners Hospital have lengthened Michael's left leg.

"They go in and they put a device in your leg and then they go in and cut the bone and, as that bone grows back, it's a very soft bone that re-grows in there, and they just stretch that."

"Is it very painful to have it done?"

"I have a very high pain tolerance."

Michael will be home this Christmas with his mother and father, Pam and Duane Comer. Their three- to four-hundred-acre family farm produces corn, beans, cattle, and pigs.

Michael's favorite food: his mother's creamy beef and macaroni followed by elderberry pie. President of his Future Farmers of America club at his high school in Greensburg, Indiana, Michael wants to be an agricultural diesel mechanic.

"Tell me a little bit about your mother and father."

"I think they've been supportive in the right way. Dad usually lets me fix stuff that's wrong at home."

"How is your walking effected?"

"It hasn't really effected me that much. I do everything. Sometimes I do even more."

"And the three toes that are gone?"

"They're just gone."

"No problem with balance?"

"No, they say you don't need toes for balance. If you don't have fingers they'll take toes and make fingers with them."

"How tall are you now?"

"I'm about five-ten, five-eleven. If I have a growth spurt I'll just come down here and they'll put a lift on the bottom of my shoe and make it taller so that my legs will be even."

"And your roommate, Juan, from Guatemala? How is he?"

"He's eighteen-years-old. He has prosthesises for an arm and leg. He was run over by a train."

Shriners Hospital for Children in Lexington does over two thousand special pediatric orthopedic procedures a year at no cost to the patient. A network of twenty-two Shriner hospitals throughout North America is funded entirely through the Shriner endowment fund, a philanthropy that has made a big difference in the life of thirteen-year-old Emily Grace Highley of Bath County.

Daughter of Pam and Eric Highley, Emily was born with scoliosis, an abnormal lateral curvature of the spine. An eighth-grader, she's had sixteen surgical procedures, including the insertion of a metal rod into her lower back. Before Christmas, another rod was planned for her upper back. "I'd be bent over without the rods," she says, smiling. Last October, Emily was wearing a "halo" with a twenty-five-pound weight to keep her neck and back straight.

"How long have you been coming here?"

"Ever since I was three."

"What is your career goal?"

"To be a small animal veterinarian."

"Will you get to go home for Christmas this year?"

"Hopefully."

Tinsel on your halo for Christmas, Emily Grace Highley! And may all children and their parents everywhere experience the joy of every season of love.

Cherish

With a name like Cherish Charles, how could she miss capturing public attention?

"Cherish" means treasure, hold dear, preserve, and nourish. It means to have respect and accept the responsibility for who you are, where you are, and what you wish to become.

Cherish Charles was born twenty-three years ago in Hazel Green, Kentucky. With a name like "Hazel Green" in a county as economically disadvantaged as Wolfe, how could educators miss such an opportunity to establish mission schools?"

Cherish, a child of the Appalachian highlands, attended a public school. Her mother, Judy, inspired her only child and Cherish became the fulfillment of a dream of excellence.

"I could not have had a better life if I had ten parents. My mother has sacrificed everything for me. She has never pushed or pressured me, but she always made it clear that the sky's the limit. When you have someone constantly encouraging you like that, you just never think to be any other way."

When Cherish speaks, the words carry a soft, resolute tone. That's how it sounded when she rose from her chair on the speaker's platform at a recent graduation ceremony at Eastern Kentucky University and delivered the commencement address to her fellow graduating students.

A 1995 graduate of Wolfe County High School, Cherish Charles made straight A's in elementary school, high school, and college. She earned a perfect 4.0 grade point average—a rare achievement.

Cherish credits her Wolfe County teachers for helping her to succeed. "There were many good teachers and many good opportunities. The schools have done the best possible job with the resources they have available."

She speaks with a maturity that sparkles. She understands what "opportunity" means: good fortune, and the chance to be helpful to others.

Cherish's major at EKU has been special education (learning and behavioral disorders). Her mother is a family service worker with Head Start.

"I have prioritized my time so that I haven't sacrificed anything," says Cherish. "I would have sacrificed a 4.0 to have a social life, but luckily I didn't have to do that. You go to class, take good notes, (and) you can do really well."

Once again, the stereotype of the unskilled, rural Kentucky woman, especially from the Appalachian highlands, has been repudiated.

"Eastern students become well-rounded individuals with an extensive sense of self," said Cherish Charles in her poised, thoughtful address at EKU's ninety-third commencement.

Those words—"well-rounded individuals" and "sense of self"— are building blocks for the future of Kentucky women. Down here, on the farm, we see more and more young people reading books and writing their own stories. They've neither pulled up their roots nor put down their parents. They've looked within themselves and have discovered new horizons.

With all the changes occurring from Wolfe to Woodford Counties, one of the most encouraging is this renewed sense of individuals choosing to break free of myths that Kentucky women are underachievers, who sometimes speak with a peculiar accent and often don't waste time with European fashions.

When my teenaged daughter and I were on a trip to France and Germany, we witnessed many of the "latest" trendsetters. From the Louvre to the Eiffel Tower, from sidewalk cafes to steep hillside vineyards, we were spellbound. But when we returned home and stepped down from the plane in home sweet Kentucky, we were grateful to be back in the state where Rhodes Scholars have risen up in places like Paintsville and Gravel Switch.

Young Kentucky women today have wonderful opportunities, and many times it begins with "going to class, taking good notes, and doing real well." Our daughter wants to become a doctor, and she was in the audience when Cherish gave her commencement address. But it takes more than doctors, more than teachers, more than religious leaders. We need skills of every kind—from piloting planes to minding plowshares.

Family is the foundation for all our activities, whether we live on the farm or in the city. That's where we learn respect for ourselves and for others. To tell you the truth, I haven't stopped for a second, being excited about being a Kentucky woman with the opportunity to leave a legacy for the next hundred years.

Cherish Charles stands tall but not alone. With the beginning of another school year, she's a role model, and her mother too is a fine example of the dedicated Kentucky woman, who sees in her daughter the hope for tomorrow.

Billy

After he was safely in his own bed, Billy realized something was completely wrong. He remembers his first words:

"What happened to all the birds?"

He was deaf.

Billy Rogers was seven years old when he returned home to Bourbon County from the hospital, too young to know he was lucky to be alive. Spinal meningitis is often fatal among infants and juveniles.

Billy was my stepbrother, and I was only five years old, so I don't recall any vivid pictures of that day, that terrible time when he went from hearing everything to hearing nothing at all. To our elders it must have been one of the most somber days of their lives. Such soul-searching questions they must have asked. They were unprepared, stunned in their disbelief.

I was living with foster parents, and nobody spoke openly about such a dreadful thing as deafness, especially in one so young.

Now in our seventies, Billy and I sat together on a recent afternoon and talked honestly about what it means to be profoundly deaf, which means unable to hear anything. The void is vast, deep as midnight along Plum Lick Creek; the Earth is fast asleep. Once, when I leaned in and asked him to repeat something, he said with a chuckle,

"What's the matter, are you hard of hearing?"

I asked him if he had a word of advice about how the state of Kentucky ought to respond to the needs of the deaf, young and old.

"Education is the key," said Billy—William Boyd Rogers—who grew up to become a farmer and then the first executive director of the Kentucky Commission on Deaf and Hard of Hearing. His father had once told me: "Get a good education, son—that's something nobody can take away from you."

Billy (some call him "Bill" but I don't know anybody who calls him "William" or "Willy.") was sent to the Pennsylvania School for the Deaf. Each summer when he returned to Kentucky we became reacquainted through the "deaf alphabet" and lip reading. I understood then, even better now, the importance of listening carefully, focusing attention, being patient when communicating with a deaf person. I remember hearing cruel taunts of "deaf and dumb" among children who chose not to understand and who believed they needed somebody to ridicule.

"Just because speech is impaired doesn't mean a deaf person can't think," said Billy.

"What are some of the more important things the hearing should understand about the hearing impaired, especially children?"

"They should realize that they are normal people and shouldn't leave them out of things. Children should learn language as soon as possible. The first year is critical."

"Early detection?"

"Yes, absolutely. It makes all the difference in the world."

Using census records of 1990, the Kentucky Commission on the Deaf and Hard of Hearing has estimated hearing loss to run as high as 10 percent.

"How many can be expected to become hard of hearing or profoundly deaf?"

"More and more," said Billy, who graduated from University High in Lexington, in 1948. Although he couldn't hear the referee's whistle or the roar of the crowd, he played on the U-High starting basketball team and went on to earn a degree in agriculture from the University of Kentucky.

Billy has campaigned for captioning on television and the Kentucky Relay Service by telephone (the number is available in the front section of the telephone book). He warns of the dangers of unprotected hearing at rock concerts and loud blasts sustained by hunters and skeet shooters. Whatever the source or occasion, deafening is a word that has a literal meaning and the potential to pass beyond temporary to permanent.

William B. Rogers urges young hearing-impaired students to attend schools—public, state, or private—where they can be with others like themselves to benefit from the interaction. "I don't know what would have happened to me if I had not," he says, at the same time encouraging lifelong involvement in the world of the hearing.

"I'm bilingual and bicultural," he smiles.

Billy has led a good and fruitful life, a role model for many others who are deaf and who have a right to full membership in the community of sound.

Logan

Meet Logan Weatherholt.

He's right on the edge of being twelve years old.

It was high time we talked to a member of the oncoming generation. Might learn something, what with all the backbiting of the retiring baby-boomer bunch.

Arrowhead hunting is Logan's love number one. He looks for them along riverbanks, especially on the Kentucky and Indiana side of the Ohio. Logan hunts with his dad, Charlie.

"Easy to find arrowheads?"

"Not easy to find...look for chipped flint or rock on the bank."

"Fish?"

"Fish all the time. Caught a twenty-pound catfish."

"Hunt?"

"Hunt deer. Two does under my belt. Use a .12-gauge or .20-gauge shotgun—kicks a little, but I'm used to it. Use a 22-rifle for squirrels."

Right away, I'm wondering about Brer Squirrel, Bambi, and guns in the hands of children.

"Hunters' education," Logan reminds us. "I have a license" to hunt and fish, he says, doubling his legs and feet up beneath himself for better thinking.

"Kill it, you eat it. Poachers shoot for the fun of it. They saw off horns. I love venison, one ninety-pound doe was sixty to seventy pounds of meat."

"Watch much television?"

"Don't watch television—interested in too many things. My mom and I sit down and paint together, oil paints. I like to draw, love to draw. I look at it, then use pencils to make different shades of gray."

Logan buys birdhouses for three dollars and sells them for twenty to thirty dollars. I look at the boy and try to remember how I was when I was close to being twelve years old.

"What do you want to become?"

"I want to be an archeologist," says Logan not missing a beat. Science and art are his favorite subjects. With A's and B's he stays on the honor roll.

"College?"

"St. Louis University. They have one of the biggest archeology teams in the nation." Logan races upstairs to his room and returns with several issues of *The Archaeological Institute of America.*

"What about zoos?"

"Don't like zoos. Don't believe in holding animals in captivity."

"Cities? What do you think about cities?"

"Don't like cities. More peaceful in the country—fresh air—the city is polluted with diesel fuel and gas, not a pretty sight. There're trees in the country and animals and the smell of fields of corn and soybeans."

When Logan was seven years old he created an oil painting, Purple Mountain Majesty. We keep reminding ourselves that this kid is eleven years old.

"What do you like to read?"

"National Geographic, Hardy Boy Books, Tom Sawyer, Huck Finn."

"Now, what about girlfriends? You have girlfriends?"

"No girlfriends. Not for me."

Well, we could remember and identify with that, but we suspected Logan could have a platoon of girlfriends if he didn't think it was more fun to hunt and fish and make money in the birdhouse trade.

"Sports? Do you like sports?

"Love sports! Basketball, baseball, football."

We the senior citizen cynics look across the table at this eleven-year-old wonder kid, and we're thinking we've been blessed to have come upon such a wonderful youth in our own twilight time, when a whole lot of geezers have retired and gone off to play shuffleboard.

"Logan, do you have a certain way of looking at the world? I mean, what would you say about your parents, but especially how you see yourself."

"My parents take care of me. I don't have to do much—mow the yard, sweep the floor, wash dishes."

"You behave?"

"I try to behave. If I'm bad, I should be disciplined."

"A final word?"

"Children should be loved...I hope you like what I do, and I'm going to stay with what I do."

With that we close our reporter's notebook, giving thanks that we don't have to call the home office and say, "No story here. Where do you want us to go next?"

Butch

From time to time, the "View from Plum Lick" back page column in Kentucky Living magazine results in a reader sitting down and writing a fine letter, too fine to savor alone. You know, it ought to be shared.

Here's to Joyce Irwin and her son, who live down in Clinton County, which is bordered on the north by Lake Cumberland and on the south by Dale Hollow Lake.

That's a whole lot of water, especially when you figure in the feeder streams—Wolf River and Illwill Creek. There's Seventy Six Falls, uncounted creeks and branches—a fisherman's paradise.

Mrs. Irwin writes:

"I enjoyed your October story about the "Inspiring youngster." It reminded me of my son so much. He too is almost twelve years old and loves to fish and hunt about as good as he loves to eat.

"My son, Butch Allen never ceases to amaze me in anything he does. With his busy hunting and fishing schedule he still remains on the honor roll.

"When he was in the fifth grade his teacher told the class they must write an essay about one of their grandparents over the weekend and that it was due early Monday morning.

"I later found out that my son told his teacher that was impossible for him to do this particular weekend that he had a full schedule that weekend between deer hunting with his dad, fishing with his Papa and church on Sunday that there was no possible way he could have the time to write an essay.

"The teacher said, 'Butch, you must take time, it's due on Monday.'

"Between his busy schedule he took the time to write the most touching story about his grandpa that a person could ever read. On January 8, 2003 (Butch's birthday) Butch Allen Irwin was announced as the winner of the 'Grandparent essay contest.'

"I hope it inspires you as much as it has for everyone who has read it."

Grandparent Essay
5th grade – 10 years old
Clinton Co. Middle School

This has been a hard decision for me to make. All my grandparents are really great to me. All of them have taught me things I will never forget.

But my grandpa or should I say 'Papa' is who I'm the closest to. We do a lot of things together, in my eyes he can 'walk on water.'

It started when I was very young, my mom and dad had to work and my nanny had to work also. So I stayed with my Papa.

My Papa is extraordinary you see, how many Papas would stay home all day and keep a one year old, play kid games, read and change diapers?

I can tell you not many, but my Papa did. As we spent many, many days together we became closer and closer. Now that I am older I help my Papa in a lot of ways, like hooking up the boat, and running the troll motor when we go fishing.

Papa and I love to go fishing. We would go fishing every day if we could and we just about do, at least every chance we get.

We spend a lot of time together while we are fishing. When we are not fishing we are talking about fishing, like the different kinds of fish we caught or the baits we used.

We were sitting on the back porch baiting our fishing poles getting them ready so when the weather is just right our fishing poles will be ready for us to load up and head out.

My Papa is a good fisherman but that's not all, he's a good listener, and good bike fixer. We like to watch all sports on T.V. together and especially fishing.

My Papa may have one bad leg but he sure has one great heart. I'm proud to call him my Papa.

By: Butch Irwin

Samanthia

When she was six years old, "the doctor looked at my mom and said 'she shouldn't be able to walk across the room without help.'"

Samanthia Farthing rose from her chair that day in the eye doctor's office, walked alone to him and said as simply and as forcefully as she knew how, "I'm God's miracle."

Now, ten years later, we went to visit sixteen-year-old Samanthia in a classroom at the non-denominational Mountain Christian Academy in Martin, just down the road from Prestonsburg in Floyd County.

"Sam" had spent the morning tutoring ten-year-olds, showing them that math is not as difficult as it seems. "People basically make math harder than it is. You can't do algebra without knowing how to multiply. Break it down and do it one step at a time."

When we put out our hand, Samanthia greeted us with a strength and smile that we could feel and instantly know was real. We sat across from each other in the room that soon would be crowded with students beginning a new fall term. Mountain Christian Academy is pre-school through the eighth grade.

Samanthia told us she'd be a junior at the nearby Catholic Piarist school, named for the 15th-century priest who dedicated his life to education reform.

Legally blind since birth, Samanthia rejects the word "handicapped." Wants no part of its meaning as "incapacitation."

"God just blessed me with independence," she says. "I can see you, but I just can't see very far. I have some peripheral vision."

When she was eighteen-months-old, Samanthia underwent surgery to uncross her eyes. "I've had all kinds of tests," she smiles, "I'm not supposed to be able to see colors, but I do. Nobody can understand why. When I was three months old, my mother would feed me with the touch of the spoon to my mouth. When she came close but didn't touch, she told me she knew I had some sight."

Samanthia remembers, when she was an early teen, she visited the School for the Blind in Louisville. "At orientation, kids were led around and being helped to do everything." As well-intended as the program was, maybe it was an inner voice that told the mountain girl to help herself, then to begin to help others.

Our conversation went beyond blindness.

"My glass is half full, not half empty," said Samanthia, drawing from a family foundation of faith.

"Do you know about Helen Keller?" We should have known better to ask.

"One of my heroes!" she replied.

"How do you see your future?"

"Social work, but I'm not sure. I'm exploring different degrees. I might work to help abused children."

Samanthia makes "mostly A's, some B's" and has earned a Robinson Creek Scholarship, which will pay for her tuition, room and board, books, and give her spending money for four years of college.

"Where will you attend?"

"The University of Kentucky," she says with a smile broadening into joy.

"Favorite subjects?"

"Math, English, and history...I don't like biology."

Samanthia finds it difficult to read Braille, and it's obvious she'd rather not.

"How about a seeing-eye dog?"

"I'd like that, because it's dangerous crossing the street."

Loneliness can be a problem, and she says she sometimes feels left out. "I can't see a concert, but I can hear it. I love to play baseball and basketball, but I can't be on the team. I attend the Little League games.

Her father manages a grocery and her mother is a pre-school teacher. Samanthia belongs to a support group, and she advises others with visual impairment "to have good friends and think of good things....You need to be happy with yourself and not pay any attention to what other people say."

We come back down the Mountain Parkway in clouds spilling rain, and we remember Samanthia's words: "I'm just God's miracle. He's my best friend and there's no way without him to lean on."

Elizabeth

Elizabeth Scoville of Laurel County celebrated her seventeenth birthday with a renewed commitment to excellence. The following spring she graduated from North Laurel High School with a grade point average of about 4.38, ranking first in a class of two hundred and seventy-two, making her the valedictorian.

Since kindergarten, Elizabeth has made nothing but A grades.

Her mother, Lawana, is a science teacher at North Laurel. Elizabeth's father, John, is a retired social studies teacher. Encouragement is a given.

Studying is a discipline.

Science is a passion.

Elizabeth Scoville is a name to remember in a new year of a new century. She's not addicted to entertainment programs on television. Says she doesn't have time to "hang out" on Friday nights. "I don't have time for boys," she smiles across the counter in the kitchen of her family's home near East Bernstadt. "One day, I'll find the right boy and if he cares enough he'll let me do what I want to do."

What Elizabeth wants to do is nanotechnology, "The science and technology of building electronic circuits and devices from single atoms and molecules." (A nanosecond is one billionth of a second.)

Stay tuned!

She's a Presidential Scholar, a Toyota scholar, and wants to become a Rhodes Scholar.

In the summer of 2005, Elizabeth was on a undergraduate research fellowship at Cincinnati Children's Hospital. It's a project dealing with ways to help newborns, especially preemies, to inflate their lungs.

After two years of 4.0 studies in Agricultural Vocational Technologies and chemistry at the University of Kentucky, Elizabeth is undecided as to whether she'll attend medical school at Duke or Washington in St. Louis.

Here we have a normal, young Appalachian woman with a purpose and a vision. Yes, Daisy Mae, Mammy Yokum, and all you other "real" Beverly Hillbillies, highly intelligent things are happening more and more in eastern Kentucky. It's time the rest of the world took notice.

Elizabeth Scoville wants to be a doctor, but she plans to move beyond the basics of childbirth, flu shots, and pacemakers. She wants to devise and develop miniature medical strategies for introduction into the molecular structure of the human body — "medically tiny machines in the blood stream giving medicine to various parts of the body," she says with her soft and confident tone of voice.

Elizabeth was five years old when she decided she wanted to be a doctor. With a toy doctor's kit she performed surgery on stuffed animals. In the eighth grade, her brother John helped her to assemble her first computer. He's now a graduate student at Stanford and works part-time at NASA.

Five years ago, Elizabeth developed a Computers for Kids Network (email: *computers_4_kids@hotmail.com*). The way it has worked, if a company or individual had aging but still working computers, Elizabeth has taken them in, checked them out, and made them available to students who had not been able to afford a computer at home. This has short-circuited landfills and the costs of dumping non-degradable lead components. Near the end of 2002, Elizabeth had processed one hundred and thirty-three computers, "Bringing schools and companies together...to give kids a chance to break the stereotypes...I feel so blessed to give a computer to a child who may not get one for Christmas."

"Computers at home are really necessary for students?"

Elizabeth smiles and nods, "Yes."

She has been president of her local Beta Club, earned the Girl Scout Gold Award, been a participant in the Kentucky's STLP, Student Technology Leadership Program, been a member of the Future Problem Solving team and student in the Governor's Scholars Program.

At home in Laurel County she studies from two to three hours— "It's been forever since I watched television"—and she has some friendly tips for students. "Never give up...train yourself for discipline...you really can do anything...but not everyone is a rocket scientist...the most important thing is to learn what you love because that's where you'll go in life...there'll always be another opportunity to 'hang out,' you can't re-do school."

Elizabeth is named for her great-great aunt, Elizabeth Jane Scoville, who taught school for more than fifty years. Riding a big red mare, she and two other women from Louisville founded one of the first schools in Owsley County. That was near the beginning of the twentieth century.

Some miracles have happened since then.

Crystal

"Being country is as much a part of me as my full lips, wide hips, dreadlocks and high cheek bones. There are many Black country folks who have lived and are living in small towns, up hollers and across knobs."

Crystal Wilkinson wrote these words in her 2000 book *Blackberries, Blackberries.*

Her Affrilachian roots are up on Indian Creek east of Turkey Knob in Casey County, Kentucky. Her first book was published when she was only fourteen years old. Now her outreach has become universal. Today, in middle age, she cherishes her Appalachian upbringing, and she's not likely to forget it, because she had quickly understood the importance of place.

"If a writer's work is defined by what she knows, then my stories have always been Black and country like me."

Crystal's grandmother knew something unusual was unfolding, and she didn't stand in the way. "She watched me from behind the screen door, my body cradled in the overgrown roots of a poplar tree going about writing like killing snakes. Her call for me to come to supper fell on deaf ears. She found me down by the creek or out by the edge of the woods at dusk in a scribbling fury.

"Once upon a time, far up a holler in the hills of Kentucky, there

Butch

From time to time, the "View from Plum Lick" back page column in *Kentucky Living* magazine results in a reader sitting down and writing a fine letter, too fine to savor alone. You know, it ought to be shared.

Here's to Joyce Irwin and her son, who live down in Clinton County, which is bordered on the north by Lake Cumberland and on the south by Dale Hollow Lake.

That's a whole lot of water, especially when you figure in the feeder streams—Wolf River and Illwill Creek. There's Seventy Six Falls, uncounted creeks and branches—a fisherman's paradise.

Mrs. Irwin writes:

"I enjoyed your October story about the "Inspiring youngster." It reminded me of my son so much. He too is almost twelve years old and loves to fish and hunt about as good as he loves to eat.

"My son, Butch Allen never ceases to amaze me in anything he does. With his busy hunting and fishing schedule he still remains on the honor roll.

"When he was in the fifth grade his teacher told the class they must write an essay about one of their grandparents over the weekend and that it was due early Monday morning.

"I later found out that my son told his teacher that was impossible of what they think good writing is. So I settled on just concentrating on writing more, not publishing.

"I decided I would not join the ranks of the factory wordsmiths who got paid high sums to crank out formula fiction. I wanted my writing to remain whole and to continue to be a reflection of 'what I know.'"

As she concluded her soul-stirring acceptance remarks, tears streaking down her peaceful, yet determined face: "...we need to write because the world wants to hear what we have to say. And my last point is that we can do it right here. We don't have to move away to do it."

This cinnamon-skinned daughter with hair as black as starling's wings has seen her first book, *Blackberries, Blackberries,* go into its third printing. Then came her second book, *Water Street*, and her third book, a novel "about Black farms in Kentucky.

"Today," says Crystal of herself as she sits in a corner in her favorite place, in her favorite room, with her favorite pen and she writes—"Is this the end of this story? No, hopefully, it's only the beginning not just for me but for all of us."

Uncle Jimmy

Just when we thought we'd lived our lives without becoming jugglers, along comes Stuart Ashman's *The Great Juggling Kit*, a wonderful high school graduation gift for our daughter, Ravy. She's now juggling college chemistry, English, marching band, boyfriends, women's choir, and rugby with eyes on her ultimate goal of becoming a nurse.

Soon-to-be ninety-four years old, "Uncle Jimmy" Harvey, who loves to play the circus clown and perform all kinds of tricks and sleights of hand, is the giver of the magic gift.

At first glance, the three blue, green, red, and yellow balls look like hardly more than colorful worry stones—pleasant to look at, relaxing to squeeze, nice to touch lightly, thereby feeling less stressed.

The kit's sixty-four-page book, published by Barnes & Noble, is loaded with pictures of young and over-the-hillers performing a skill as olden as medieval time, even thousands of years ago in Ancient Egypt when entertainment was always catch-as-catch-can.

Clutching and releasing the three (or more) balls, keeping them constantly

172

in motion, requires unbroken concentration. (Professional jugglers can manage five balls—eleven is the world record.) Up until now, we were childish enough to think that jugglers were born with this ability. It didn't occur to us that it's something that can be learned beginning with the fundamentals—the "jugglespace," "cascade," "top of the arc," "the snatch," "chop," "shower," and "the Statue of Liberty." (Juggling has its own vocabulary; there's not enough space here to explain each meaning.)

One thing we've noticed is that jugglers are almost always smiling, which causes others to lose frowns. Being a good juggler is handy when times are rough and traveling with the circus or college crowd is one of the few acts in or out of town.

Here's a game plan idea for teenagers and senior citizens: juggling is what we do every day, the big difference is deciding what oranges to toss and catch and what lemons to forget about right from the get-go.

It doesn't do much good to juggle indecision, procrastination, and down-and-out laziness. Does it? Better to juggle the reading of three good books than three bad books. Better to juggle the watching of three good television programs instead of three bad television programs. Makes more sense to juggle time to accommodate three interesting and challenging people rather than wasting time bowing and scraping for three people who hinder more than they help.

Right?

The Great Juggling Kit has taught us to begin with one thing, build up to two, and then move on to three things. Who knows? Maybe we can learn to do four or five things at the same time: have a career, family, and spiritual life. Or, we could reverse the order. Compensate. Maybe work in a hobby. Build a circle of friendships. Volunteer. Be true to ourselves. It's the flow that matters. Smooth flow. Well-timed release, catch, release, catch. Coordination.

What applies to the sighted, works for the visually challenged. We have a friend, Michael, blind from birth, who teaches music, mimics other voices, and practices basketball free throws in his backyard. Another friend, Bonnie, has no arms but drives a car with her feet, waves goodbye with her toes, and wears a watch on her ankle. Another friend, Willie, has no legs, but drives a car with his hands and, pushing his wheelchair loaded with fishing equipment, walks on his knees to the edge of a lake. These three juggle life better than we ever will.

There's an International Jugglers Association, a magazine called *Juggle*, and an *Encyclopedia of Ball Juggling*, and a *Compendium of Club Juggling*. There's even something called siteswap on the Internet, where jugglers can swap patterns by using a complex numbering scheme.

We tend toward seeing the practical in just about everything. If it will cause us to relax, smile, and move smoothly through another day without harm to ourselves and others, then we're the happiest clowns on the face of this old earth—spinning through a universe of juggling stars!

Lot

Pulling into the parking lot, I was careful not to occupy a space for which I was not entitled. Really bugs me to see an ignored "Handicap Only" sign, especially when the offender is young and full of beans.

Picking my way across the icy patches and up the front steps of the assisted living/nursing home, I was reminded that some of us aren't as spry as we used to be. Some of us can't afford to stumble.

Navigating the corridors, past the open doors—faces lighting up with expectation of a family visitor, others darkened and drawn by too many disappointments.

"Good afternoon," I say to a passing nurse.

"Good afternoon," is the cheerful reply.

An attendant asks a resident seated in a wheelchair, "May I push?"

"Yes, you may," is the soft and appreciative reply. And down the hallway they go, stopping at an apartment.

"Here you are!"

I hear the act of kindness, then move on to find Mr. Lot Richart Henry's door, and I knock.

"Come in," his sturdy voice resonates.

Mr. Henry lives alone in a two-room apartment.

He's ninety years old.

Seated in his favorite chair, he's wearing a dress shirt and neatly knotted tie. He's waiting for me. We'd agreed I would come after he'd finished his lunch. Cold slaw and green beans are two of his favorite dishes.

We shake hands, as is the custom upon arriving and departing, opening and closure statements of trust. The reason for our new friendship: the sharing of bygone names and places in the little community where we spent our childhoods.

"Named for the doctor who delivered me."

"Lot is your first name?"

"Biblical. Went to a carnival once. Fortuneteller said she'd bet a dollar she could tell me my name. Said, 'Concentrate on your name.' I concentrated on 'Richart' because that's what everybody called me. Most said 'Richard,' and I wouldn't care. Figured I'd won an easy dollar from this fortuneteller.

"She rubbed her hands all over this big crystal ball and finally she said, 'I'm not getting anything.' Are you sure you're concentrating on your first name?'"

Richart switched to his first name "Lot," same as Abraham's nephew.

"She rubbed her hands over that crystal ball, then pointed her finger at me and said, 'Lot. Your name is Lot!'"

Lot Richart Henry and I had a real good laugh, and we both felt better. We fell right into the time when the man was murdered on a certain road, because he had insulted somebody, to the man who would grab your ears and nearly twist them off, to that first chew of tobacco, to the young lady who "is still beautiful," to fifteen cents a gallon gasoline, to teachers coming and going.

"I set a trap for rabbits and one time on my

way to school I reached in and pulled out a polecat. Well, I turned loose of him as fast as I could, but by the time I'd taken my seat in the schoolhouse the teacher said, 'Somebody in here's got skunk on 'em. Who is it?'

"I raised my hand. She said, 'Well of all people.' So, I got up and walked out."

We had ourselves another good laugh. We took up the fine art of hoboing, regrettable dove hunts on baited fields, shooting squirrels, the interurban to Lexington, being right-handed but always putting on the left shoe first, not living with your children when you get to be 90, learning how not to eat too much.

"Push back," said Abraham's nephew. "No second helpings and don't make the first one too big. It's all in your head."

I said I'd give it a try.

I arose to leave, we shook hands, and I realized how fortunate I was.

I could walk.

Lot Richard Henry can stand and ease himself into his motorized wheelchair. That's all. But he has a remarkable, special gift of memory despite his inability to move his feet—his brain is better motorized that his chair!

We waved.

"See you next time!"

Abe

There's a story told about Abe when he was president of the United States. Seems he was holding a cabinet meeting, and the discussion became unnecessarily catawampus. Lincoln finally just up and asked, "How many legs would a dog have if you called the tail a leg?"

There was a pause.

Much thought.

Careful political head scratching. Diplomatic toe turning. Then, somebody said, "Well, Mr. President, it would be five."

"No," said the man who began his life on a farm in Kentucky. "It would still be four. Calling a tail a leg doesn't make it a leg."

Calling a false statement a truth, a disparity an agreement, or a school an education fall approximately into the same category.

Abe was born February 12, 1809, near the South Fork of Nolin River, but his boyhood home was on the edge of Knob Creek, a tributary of Rolling Fork, both places in LaRue County. These streams are a vital part of the great water engine and make Kentucky so unusual (more miles of navigable waterways than any state in the union, except Alaska).

Thomas, Nancy Hanks, Abe, and sister Sarah moved to Knob Creek in the spring of 1811. Carl Sandberg described the place in his book, *Abraham Lincoln*. "That Knob Creek farm in their valley set round by high hills and deep gorges was the first home Abe Lincoln remembered....He scrawled words with charcoal, he shaped them in the dust, in sand, in snow. Writing had a fascination for him."

Today, teachers are required to force writing portfolios into the consciousness of sleeping Abes and Abigales. A prime-time reason for it is the easy availability of video—movies and television—and internet sleights of hand.

Too often this is true on snow days when there is no school. Instead of reading by the fireside or at the kitchen table, students and parents hover and seek warmth from the television set(s). It's like a "free" vacation, and the post-Lincoln age habitually resists learning as much as Abe longed for it.

The same power that produced the Great Emancipator continues to create opportunities throughout Kentucky. Good people can still reach for the stars, drawing from within themselves, trusting in authentic intuition, relying on values derived naturally, not artificially from the media entertainment centers of Hollywood, New York, and Washington, D.C.

The birth month of the sixteenth President of the United States is a good time to reflect upon the life of Lincoln and how it is to be growing up today in Kentucky. A promising start would be to read Sandberg's book, which could lead to David Donald's *Lincoln Reconsidered*. An idea for spring might include a visit to Lincoln country—Hodgenville and Knob Creek. Go and listen. Take along a candle and a book in case there's no power outlet.

It has been more than ironic that Kentucky is the birthplace of the two opposing presidents in the American Civil War. Eight months older than Lincoln, Jefferson Davis was born June 3, 1808, in what is now Todd County. Both he and Lincoln were as reviled as they were revered. Perhaps, Kentuckians will find increased understanding of Davis by reading Robert Penn Warren's *Jefferson Davis Gets His Citizenship Back*.

A short reading list should include Frederick Douglass's *Life and Times*, Booker T. Washington's *Up from Slavery*, and James Baldwin's *Go Tell It On the Mountain*.

The point of all this is not to push the envelope of politically correctness, engage in hero worship, or open old wounds. The main thought is to encourage reading, then writing, at each stage of a lifetime of learning.

Winter is a good time to put another log on the fire and to ponder the depth and breadth of the process of our education as individuals. Neither Lincoln, Davis, Douglass, Washington, nor Baldwin allowed others to do their thinking for them, nor should we.

PART
Three

When you're in a Kentucky state of mind,
There's no telling what might jump and
kiss you on the top of the head!

Monkey's Eyebrow

$\mathcal{M}$onkey's Eyebrow reminds us of Plum Lick—if you're flying by the seat of your road map, you could zip right through it and never know you'd been there.

When you're in the Kentucky state of mind, there's no telling what might jump up and kiss you on the top of the head.

In the case of Plum, most around here in Bourbon County, even in the fruitiest of times, don't call it Plum. Most call it "The Levy" (not to be confused with the possibly more correctly spelled "Levee" in adjoining Montgomery County). We've yet to have it on best authority as to how either place got its name.

Tradition has it that Plum got its name from plum seeds spit out by Native Americans in hunting parties on their way to and from the Ohio River. We question the authenticity of this theory, because if it were true, there'd been Plums all over the neighborhood. One of most signposts is enough.

Leads to less confusion.

What counts are the people and the here and now. What happened yesterday and what might transpire tomorrow aren't nearly as important as what's staring us right in the face. The present winks, the past nods, the future yawns.

As it is, there are many interesting place names to visit in

PLUM LICK PUBLISHING

P. O. Box 68   North Middletown KY 40357-0068

(859) 383-4366 Telephone

Website: www.kyauthors.com   Email: DDick@kyauthors.com

David and Lalie Dick
personally sign & inscribe all books to order!

Kentucky-A State of Mind	*Jesse Stuart-The Heritage*	*Rivers of Kentucky*
...storytelling with a dash of tall-tale telling. A reminder that the land stretching across Kentucky is rich in humor and self worth....a nonfiction book paying tribute to the individual, laying to rest the stereotypes.	...a bold, imaginative biography of the poet, novelist, short-story writer, and teacher. Jesse Stuart comes to life once more through hitherto unpublished personal correspondence with family, mentors, and friends.	...a treasure-trove of non-fiction information and lore about this North American place called Kentucky. As varied in style and content as the Kentucky landscape, it is an atlas, a guidebook and a story collection rolled into one.
Home Sweet Kentucky	*The View from Plum Lick*	*The Scourges of Heaven*
...over 90 nonfiction essays to slow you down, warm your heart, and lift you up. It'll take you to many forgotten places, introduce you to people who generally don't make headlines and give you a taste of the *essence* of	...one of Kentucky's most treasured collections of nonfiction essays... it continues to warm hearts and win friends throughout the world. A magical elixir and the world will feel better about itself for having read it.	...a historical novel of prejudice and plague, this spellbinding novel sweeps gracefully, joyfully, painfully across centuries and generations. More powerfully told than any factual account could ever manage, with a central theme of hope.
Follow The Storm	*Peace at the Center*	*The Quiet Kentuckians*
...based in part on detailed journals kept through much of David Dick's news career, a compelling story of a quest for truth and of a search for the joy to be found in human connections and love of the earth.	...a singular message that personal peace is available for those who are sensitive to the signals of life, this collection of essays is must reading for everyone seeking an understanding of living and satisfaction of life.	...rooted in the values of real people in little places doing important things but receiving little recognition, it embodies truths as seen in the lives and heard in the voices of these self-reliant, *individuals*.

We personally inscribe all books to order!

Qty.	Description	Amt.
	Kentucky—A State of Mind by David & Lalie Dick—288 pages, illustrated ISBN 0-9755037-1-5 (hard bound) $22.00	
	Jesse Stuart—The Heritage A Biography by David Dick—312 pages w/photos ISBN 0-9755037-0-7 (hard bound) $24.95	
	Rivers of Kentucky by David & Lalie Dick—288 pages, illustrated ISBN 0-9632886-8-7 (hard bound) $22.00	
	The Quiet Kentuckians by David Dick—260 pages, illustrated ISBN 0-9632886-4-4 (hard bound) $22.00	
	The Scourges of Heaven by David Dick—332 pages, illustrated ISBN 0-81312074.8 (soft bound) $19.95	
	Home Sweet Kentucky by David & Lalie Dick—260 pages, illustrated ISBN 0-9632886-7-9 (hard bound) $18.95	
	Follow The Storm: A Long Way Home by David Dick—288 pages, illustrated ISBN 0-9632886-9-5 (hard bound) $23.95	
	Peace at the Center by David Dick—242 pages, illustrated ISBN 0-9632886-2-8 (hard bound) $17.95	
	The View from Plum Lick by David Dick—256 pages, illustrated ISBN 0-9632886-6-0 (hard bound) $22.00	
	Subtotal	
	Kentucky residents, please add 6% sales tax	
	S & H: $2.50 f/1st. book, $.50 ea. addn'l. book	
	TOTAL READING PLEASURE	

Ship To:

( ) check or Money Order Enclosed   ( ) Bill Me

Please charge to my MasterCard or VISA

Card #   Exp Date ___/___

Telephone #

Signature

Name(s) to whom books are to be inscribed, or additional inscription information

Telephone & Email orders welcome!

Kentucky and so little time to get to all of them: Illwill Creek in Clinton County, Possum Trot in Marshall County, Lick Skillet in Livingston County, Bugtussle in Monroe County, and Tywhapity Bottoms on the Hancock-Daviess County line. (Robert M. Rennick's *From Red Hot to Monkey's Eyebrow: Unusual Kentucky Place Names.*)

Red Hot is in Greenup County in the area north of Warnock near the juncture of KY 2 and KY 7. Rennick tells the story of how Red Hot got its name, a good read, and it hand-delivered to the author a dandy title for his book.

Which brings us back full circle to Monkey's Eyebrow.

We figured our "been there, done that" list would not have been complete without a trip to Monkey's Eyebrow. So, we followed U.S. 60 west from Paducah toward something called Future City and West Future City. Just like Plum, we were into the future and out of the future without ever knowing the present or the past, which should have been sufficient warning—some maps and storytellers have been known to promise more than they deliver.

On across the McCracken-Ballard County line through Kevil, where we could have stopped for our baloney sandwich, but we were hell-bent to find our way to Monkey's Eyebrow.

We took a shortcut around La Center, headed north on KY 358 to the juncture with KY 1782, then headed west through Needmore and finally arrived at what we believed to be Monkey's Eyebrow.

Other than a television relay tower and a taxidermy shop (no comparison intended), the best part of Monkey's Eyebrow was well-tended Ohio River bottom land, neatly trimmed yards, and nicely

painted homes with plenty of space for everybody's state of mind. Nobody in a hurry—in fact, nobody in sight.

No gridlock.

No dings.

No honking horns.

Not in Monkey's Eyebrow.

Maybe the name comes from the shape of the Ohio River at this point, or it could have been a riverboat captain making a toast: "Here's to your Monkey's Eyebrow." Can't be too sure.

On our way back east to Paducah, we celebrated by stopping for a baloney sandwich at Hughes's Grocery on the Ogden Landing Road. Allan Hughes fixed us up.

What a treat! Nothing fancy. Just non-threatening talk about the best way to call a wild turkey, being responsible in the hunting season, and not worrying about trying to get ahead of the next feller. Plenty of smiles and heartfelt expressions that seemed to say, "Come back and spend more time when you think you can."

Let's just put it this way: when we get plum worn out with Plum Lick, we'll seriously consider moving to Monkey's Eyebrow, if they'd have us there.

And they probably would

No Baloney

Like a ghost on a stormy night, the question arises: "Was your first baloney sandwich story, which you made to sound like the beginning of all creation, was that story real? Did it actually happen? Or did you just make it up whole cloth? Were you just funnin'? That's what we want to know."

"Only some of the names were changed to protect the guilty," I reply and go on about the business of whittling a favorite stick of cedar.

I recall, as if it were only yesterday, but it was roughly fifty years ago, Joe Creason was sitting sideways at his desk against the wall on the fourth floor of *The Courier-Journal* building in Louisville. I'd come down from the sixth floor where the WHAS Radio and Television newsroom was located.

"Joe, I'm going down to Barkley County (there is no Barkley County in Kentucky) to do a little documentary, need some contacts, thought you might help."

"Frolic Fain at Caninesville," said Joe, who knew Kentucky like the lines in the palm of his hand. "Ask him for one of his baloney sandwiches and he'll set you in the right direction."

If there was anything that stood out about Mr. Fain and his grocery store it was the spit-polish shine on his meat-cutting machine. Mr. Fain's meat-cutting machine was as clean as a hound's tooth. For miles around there might be unspeakable littering — beer cans to abandoned refrigerators, junk cars to busted bedsprings — inside Flolic Fain's store, the meat-cutting machine was enough to have made the poets proud. If you looked at it too long it would make you blink. You could part your hair by what you saw in the surface of the meat-cutting machine.

"Mr. Fain, I'm from Louisville. Joe Creason said I should look you up."

"Did?"

"Yessir, he did. You see, I'm doing this television documentary on the hydroelectric project. Joe said you had the best baloney sandwiches between here and Louisville."

Mr. Fain turned to the refrigerator, reached inside and took out a long tube of baloney that looked like it'd been made in baloney heaven. He walked to the meat-cutting machine and threw the switch. That meat-cutting machine hummmmed like the sweet juice of glory. The blade turned in anticipation that it was about to do what it was meant to do since the coming of the Industrial Revolution.

Frolic Fain's sure hand eased the tube of baloney toward the blade. When they touched, it was divine consummation. "Scrooommm," they touched, and one slice lay over like a ballet dancer touching her toes. "Scrooommm," and the second slice joined the first, a pas de deux to have made Dame Fonteyn proud.

Frolic gathered the two slices, married them between two slices of light bread and laid the critter on the counter. He stood back and smiled. I bit into the sandwich and smiled back. Of such encounters do lasting friendships take root and grow with never backward glance.

A few weeks later, I returned to Barkley County to do some clean-up work on my forgettable, one-man television documentary. I made several of those during my time at WHAS, and none cried out for Pulitzers or Emmys.

It was a hot summer day in Caninesville, and when I arrived at the crossroads I was more thirsty for a soft drink than I was hungry for another baloney sandwich. Wouldn't you know it? Frolic Fain's store was closed. There was a sign on the door, "Back in thirty minutes." There was nothing to do but wait. I looked for some shade on the side of the building, and that's where I came upon a sorry dog, an ugly dog, sleeping and snoring as if there were no tomorrow.

While many will serve up turkey and dressing, light rolls, cranberry sauce, and apple pie with a big scoop of homemade ice cream melting on top, some of us like to settle for something simpler and a lot less trouble. We purists prefer our baloney sandwiches naked, plain without insulting mustard or distracting pickle relish. The purist of the pure even leave off the superfluous bread.

This true story is dedicated to Joe Creason, one of Kentucky's beloved tall tale tellers. Joe was born in 1918 in Marshall County, and died in 1974 in Louisville, where for many years he wrote a column for *The Courier-Journal* called "Joe Creason's Kentucky." Joe is buried in Bath County, just a few miles from Plum Lick.

The first trip was a success. Baloney sandwich—great!

Second trip? Well, let's tell it like it actually happened, fulfilling the prophesy that a reporter will do almost anything to get "the story."

You see, this sleeping, flea-bitten dog was quivering and snoring by the side of Frolic Fain's grocery store at Caninesville crossroads (names made up to protect the guilty).

He was one of the ugliest dogs I'd ever seen in a lifetime of admiring all kinds of dogs. This was a scroungy dog. His ribs showed. When he breathed, little puffs of dust rose up and settled back down on his crusted nose. He was a Camelot for fleas — reminded me of an old crumpled throw rug that had spent more time outside the house than in it.

About this time, Frolic Fain returned in his pickup truck. At the sound of the engine, this good-for-hardly-anything hound jumped up like he'd been shot from a cannon or maybe just launched on a space mission to Mars. His target was the front door, and by the time Frolic had his hand on the knob, that dog had his crusted old nose snug up to the crack in the doorjamb. His nose vibrated like a dust devil, throwing off tiny, fine flecks of dog powder shimmering in the sunlight, slanting across the tree tops, finding their home of homes on Frolic Fain's doorstep.

When Frolic opened the door, that dog took off running down the front of the counter like he was at the head of the stretch at the West Memphis dog track. He was going and blowing. He rounded the counter corner, all four legs tangling and untangling. He headed up the backside of the counter like a dog who knew where he was headed on a day meant to be and it had finally come to pass.

He was going full-tilt boogie until he reached the take-no-prisoners meat-cutting machine.

That's when he threw on the brakes.

He jumped up, put both scrawny front paws on the edge of the meat-cutting machine and licked the whole thing, clean as a whistle.

Frolic Fain smiled and said, "Bet you want another baloney sandwich."

I smiled back and said, "Yep, reckon I do."

Catahoula

What do you get when you cross a German shepherd with a Doberman pinscher?

According to one legend going back to the sixteenth century, military leaders in Europe crossed the two breeds and what resulted came to be known as the indomitable European War Dog.

We're talking some kind of dawg.

Not your everyday lap snuggler.

Modern historians of the breeds may dismiss this folk tale as far-fetched, so anybody with a better version is encouraged to throw it over the fence.

The way we heard it, Charles V (1500-58), ruler of Spain and Spanish America, used these War Dogs to help drive the French out of Italy, conquer Tunis, and defeat Barbarossa, the terror of the Mediterranean.

The conquered must have had a sneaking suspicion they were up against the hounds of Hades, because the European War Dog was seldom in a mood to take prisoners.

According to the story written by the late R.T. Bonnette, newspaper reporter near Catahoula Parish in Louisiana, there was a nineteen-year-old soldier in Emperor Charles' army who took several litters of European War Dogs to Peru. This was back in the time of

Francisco Pizarro, conqueror of the Inca Empire. The dogs played a fanged role in it and when Spain annexed Cuba (Pizarro became the first governor), the War Dogs were there too. They went wherever there was a need for courage, strength, cunning, and terrible speed.

In 1539, it was a short boat ride to Florida with Fernando De Soto, and the War Dogs went along. De Soto was as hungry for an empire of gold as most all dogs dream of bone Heaven. The famous explorer anchored in Tampa Bay with six hundred men and about one hundred War Dogs.

Two years later, De Soto finally reached the Mississippi River, crossed it, didn't find the Promised Land, was wounded in a battle with Indians, contracted a fever, and died. His men weighted his body, and dropped it into the river so that it could not be found.

As the explorers straggled south, they failed to gather up all the War Dogs. According to Cajun Bonnette, the warrior's best friend wandered in the wilderness and had the good sense to survive by obeying natural instincts.

So, what do you get when you cross a European War Dog with a wolf?

You get a Catahoula Cur named for the Catahoula Indians in what is now Catahoula Parish, Louisiana.

Which brings us home to Alvin "Dub" and Judy Allen, consummate breeders of the Kentucky Catahoula Stock Dog formerly of Bourbon County: "Broke dogs, puppies and started dogs—will help you pen your cattle and work your cattle. Problem-cattle caught."

On a Sunday afternoon in late winter, it's a joy to sit with Dub and Judy surrounded by their fifteen award-winning Catahoulas (not counting the litter nursing in the back room).

Judy thinks of Red Dog and sighs: "He works so quickly and so beautifully and he's got this husky sounding voice, and he works and makes your hair stand up on your arms."

"There ain't no pain in these dogs...there ain't no such thing as pain," says Dub, recalling Spike. "I've worked them ten or twelve hours, all day long."

"What bonds you to these dogs?"

"Their intelligence...it makes the cattle so much easier to handle. With these dogs here it ain't no problem. I can pull a trailer right out here in the field and load up the cattle right there."

By their double glassy eyes you'll dern sure remember the Catahoula Cur. Depth of stare. Round head. Loyalty and commitment to the notion that tough jobs require tough dogs.

Judy says, "When they look at me with those eyes, they make me feel like I'm the only thing on this earth."

Speed? The warning hanging on the back rampart speaks volumes: "I can get to the fence in three and a half seconds. How fast can you?"

We went home and let the years slide by. Dub and Judy moved away, and we let our Catahoula Cur dreams vanish in the mist of our love for all kinds of dogs.

We took in a Labrador-chow puppy dropped in our driveway. He had a kink in his tail, so we named him "Kink."

We wondered if that name might become an uncomplimentary "Kinky," but that has not happened even once. Sometimes, we call him "Buddy Boy," "Mister Buddy," or "My Main Man."

This castaway orphan settled in with Pumpkin, our senior citizen Australian shepherd. We figure Pumpkin is one hundred and five years old in dog time. She let "Mister Buddy" know right off that age has its advantages—Pumpkin is first in line for all treats, and she eats first at the automatic feeder and drinks first at the water bowl. She does not give dibs to any "Buddy Boys," "Mister Buddies," or goodness knows, any "Kinks."

Pumpkin and Kink are the oddest of odd couples. Both are "fixed," but they are no less territorial and protective. While not vicious, both have big hearts and a state of mind that says, "This is our home, and you might as well know, that's a fact."

Then there's the inside presence, Duff, an animal shelter refugee. He's a downsized poodle with a mouth as sharp as steel shutters. Duff has worked his way into the heart and soul of the lady who feeds him and provides special treats.

She tucks him in every night.

What is this dog-human connection?

A mystery.

A yearning.

Loyalty and trust.

Bonding and blessing.

But, inevitably, there's a heavy, terrible price to pay. The puppy begins irresistibly with lots of kisses but, all too soon, the aging process takes its toll.

We have a friend, Jackie Larkins, who has been the illustrator for our books and our columns. We remember so well the day when Jackie showed us his new puppy, Jake. He was a perfect little Lassie, and they were made for each other. Their happiness was remarkable. The years went by and finally we received an aching, handwritten letter from Jackie.

Jake

"Jake has died.

"He died on January 8th around 11:40 a.m. from complications of arthritis, hip dysplasia, and kidney failure.

"My sadness is profound.

"Around the first of December Jake slipped on a ramp and lost the use of his rear legs. He couldn't even stand without help. I bought a device to help hold his rear end up and to help hold his weight up and that helped some.

"But it took two of us and sometimes three people to get him up and outside to go to the bathroom. He developed sores which we doctored and healed. He got internal infections and had hyperthyroidism and had a knee that went bad.

"I would have had the knee replaced but he just got too sick.

"Mom and Dad helped me with him, taking him out and taking care of him while I was at work. He weighed one hundred and fourteen pounds.

"I bought him one of those dog wheelchairs. He used it a couple of times but didn't like it. I was trying everything to help him. I built two ramps at Mom and Dad's house so we could take him out easier.

"The night before he died he was seriously ill. He threw up all night and couldn't lie still. I was up with him all night.

"We had to take him to see the vet on the 8th on a stretcher. He could hardly walk even with our help. His leg with the bad knee swelled up the size of two. He became even more ill after we took him in. The doctor did a blood test and determined he was into kidney failure.

"The saddest moment of my life was when I heard those words.

"He said they could keep him alive maybe another week on IVs, a week and a half at most. He was suffering so much I gave the O.K. to have him put to sleep.

"I thought I would never be able to do that—but he was just so ill and in pain. I still am not sure whether it was the right thing to do even though the vet said I made the right decision.

"He said God had determined it was Jake's time and this would let him go with dignity. I just don't know.

"Three weeks earlier I switched vets to get Jake better care. At that time the vet did the same kidney failure blood test and it came back Jake did not have kidney failure. That was the single happiest moment of my life knowing he didn't have kidney failure.

"About three months ago someone asked me what was the happiest moment of my life, and I honestly could not think of one. Now I have one.

"When Jake was about one-year old, maybe eight months, I took him to obedience school. One of our things to do was run through an obstacle course. You know, weaving through cones, running through a tube, things like that. One of the obstacles was a ramp leading up to a narrow bridge that was about eight inches wide and eight feet long. A lot of dogs balked at going across.

"Not Jake.

"He looked at me, paused and then went right across as I led him. Later the instructor said she could tell from the look on his face that he trusted me. She said, "He trusts you" and knows you would not make him do anything that would hurt him.

"When Jake was on the stretcher in the vet's office I thought of those words as he looked me in the eyes.

"He trusts you.

"And I thought maybe he trusts me to end his pain and suffering.

"I'll never forget the way he looked at me.

"Jake left this world with me and Mom and Dad gathered in front of his eyes, petting him and telling him what a good boy he was and how much we loved him.

"We buried him in one of his favorite spots in the front yard at Mom and Dad's place in Eubank.

"I go out and talk to him every day.

"Mom and Dad have been having an especially hard time. Jake and Mom had grown very close the past four years. Her hearing is very bad. Jake helped her through it, letting her know when someone was at the door or when the dryer timer was sounding—with his bark.

"He was her ears.

"I miss him so much. Not a minute goes by I'm not thinking of him. He died just two months short of his eleventh birthday. He was in ninety-five percent of the editorial cartoons I did for the newspaper. I have decided to no longer do cartoons. It's just too sad now.

"Well I just wanted you both to know you are such good friends. Thank you for the nice letter you sent a while back.

"I hope you are all doing well.

"Good health to you and your dogs.
Jackie."

Town Hall Meeting

"Gather 'round all you dogs, I've got an important announcement."

"O.K., Boss, but do we get a treat first?" said Mr. Buddy, switching his sharply kinked tail on one end and showing us his black-splotched, pink tongue on the other.

"Yeah, Boss, did I hear the treat word?" muttered one hundred and five-year-old Pumpkin, whelped in southwestern Mississippi, living out her glory years working cattle and Kink in Kentucky.

"Treat? Treat? Treat?" pitter-pattered Duff, the fluffy little poodle saved from the recesses of the humane society.

"No treat until you hear the announcement, because after you hear it, you might want to consider leaving Dog Town."

"Boss, you ain't puttin' us back on the road, by any bad chance, 'er ye?" said Kink taking aim on a tick.

"Whoa back, Boss," said Pumpkin in a low and even groan, "Don't be teasing us about the treat thing. You know how we live for it—I, the senior person being first in line, do not appreciate being fooled with—I, Pumpkin—the in-your-face, nose-tweekin', heel-nippin', head-'em-up-and-git-'em to the loading pens, fearless, faithful, evermore-on-time cattle mover—do not, I say, do not play around with the treats at the end of my illustrious, long career."

"Dern, Pumpkin, how you do get worked up when it's time for old wimmen dogs to be a-listenin',," said Kink, eyes sparkling, crooked tail wagging, moisture moving across the dark spots on his hungered tongue.

"Yip, yip, yip," chattered Duff, "Treat now, announcements later."

"Thank you for your various contributions here in Dog Town, my darlings, but the announcement comes first.

You could have heard a flea flutter at the town hall meeting.

"I have decided to bring in a Catahoula Cur—does anybody have anything they want to say about it?"

"Say what?" sputtered Kink.

"Surely not one of them," groaned Pumpkin.

"Treat, treat, treat," sputtered Duff.

"Listen up. We've got a coyote problem, as you know and, so far, none of you is doing anything about it except a precious few, pitiful, low-level howlings at the moon. One of these times, a hungry coyote is going to come in here and take his pick—a juicy Kink, a cured Pumpkin, or a cream puff Duff. Now, we wouldn't want that, would we?"

"The boss is on to something," said Kink, clearing his throat.

"Go on," said Pumpkin, "We've heard the good news, there's got to be some bad."

"Treat, treat, treat," said Duff.

"The only possible bad news is that I'm bringing in a dog named Cat."

"You what?"

"Say it ain't so, Boss."

"Treat, treat..."

"Shut up, you animal shelter lottery winner."

"The three of you should be grateful that Dog Town exists. You're well fed and patted on the head. All medical expenses are covered. In short, you have a home. Now, it appears to your boss that some additional help is in order.

"Cat is a Catahoula Cur puppy from central Louisiana. She's a crazy-eyed, white, gray, black-spotted critter descended from a long line of wild hog hunters."

"She what?" swallowed Kink.

"Sounds like Dog Town's about to become Trouble Town," said Pumpkin.

"Treat..."

"Will you cool it, Mr. Pampered? The boss is looking out for us. So, shut up and listen or I'm going to give you something to write home about to the shelter—turn you from poodle to puddle."

"All right, I've checked out Cat, and when she gets here, I suggest you make her welcome and see if you can stay out of her way. She's just a six-week-old puppy, but this time next year she'll outweigh all of you. If you see any coyotes moving through, you might just mention, Dog Town has become Cat Town, devil take the hind most.

"Now, the treats!"

The dogs smiled.

"We gonna keep our eyes open," said Kink.

A Dog Named Cat

When we picked up the dog named "Cat" we knew we had a new beginning.

We'd needed a puppy fix. Badly.

Needed a wiggly to wrap itself around our weary hearts.

Needed four promising paws to grow into dog-hood, and to dig into the domain we call home.

We'd decided we needed no German shepherd like Dirk of bygone days. No rottweiler named Chief. No Charplaninatz like Lady. No Great Pyrenees like Lamb Dawg. No border collie like Chip, nor Irish setter named Patricia. Nor dachshound the likes of Turkey.

We needed a different point of view, a dramatically different perspective for the challenges of a new dog-day. The situation definitely cried out for a Catahoula.

We had tried to explain the matter to Pumpkin, Kink, and Duff—present members of our canine confederation, but they must have thought we were kidding.

They were not prepared for the dog named Cat.

"Pumpkin, this is Cat. Kink, this is the new kid on the block. Her name is Cat. Duff, this Cat is, as you can see, already almost as big as you are. Remember, you are not going to be any taller. You have reached the limit of your standing in the sun, little poodles being little poodles."

Duff muttered, "This ain't no treat."

Cat's new home was to be the wooden doghouse with the roof of asphalt shingles, a special place where no other creature dared to tread. Down the road, this would include any marauding coyotes.

At this puppy moment, Cat could have made a delicious bon-bon for a hungry mama or daddy coyote. They'd been sending up after-midnight screams, piercing the darkened air up and down Plum Lick Creek.

"Cat, you need to be careful, don't press your European War Dog/wolf genes too far. Maybe you should practice bravery on Kink and let it go at that. I mean, you're just a babe in the woods, and we don't want you to wind up being coyote candy."

Cat must've understood. Her clear, light aqua blue/pink eyes fixed on Kink like he was a good moving target for practice. She made a snap of her head and fired off a round of Catahoula Cur wildness. Kink pivoted and proceeded rapidly to find the other side of the paint-flaking meat house.

Cat looked around with her Catahoula stare as if to say, "Laissez les bons temps rouler...let the good times roll."

As soon as we set Cat on the ground, she took turns chasing the other three dogs as if they were toys to be chewed.

Pumpkin, in her aging way, tolerated the menace with motherly disdain. Duff was caught off guard and could not do much more than tighten a circle like a wagon train taking evasive action. Kink was totally out of sorts, growing up in the middle of Pumpkin mothering and Duff silliness. Now, the black-tongued orphan was being chased by a young warrior bent on proving that there were new scores to be settled.

Kink was not immediately pleased.

Peeking around the corner of the above-ground cellar, he re-thought his predicament. The dog named Cat was taking her work as seriously as a young bumblebee in flowering wisteria.

Kink must've thought it was now or never. He marched in a straight line toward Cat's quivering backside and before you could say Catahoula three times, Kink bit down on the puppy's head like a vise looking for a wooden two-by-four. Adding insult to injury, Kink pierced Cat's right ear, a little extra touch she will everlastingly remember—in the fullness of time she will extract retaliation (if Kink should dare to live so long).

Cat screamed loud enough to scare a den full of hungry coyotes. She floundered her way to the doghouse, limped inside, and dreamed of better days to come.

J. LARKINS

more

Patriotism

"Give me liberty or give me death!" said Patrick Henry, the great patriot of the American Revolution—but liberty to do what?—aye, there's the rub.

Lord Bolingbroke wrote: "Patriotism must be founded in great principles, and supported by great virtues." But, more definitions are needed with the introduction of principle and virtue.

Whose principle?

Whose virtue?

How much support?

According to Dr. Samuel Johnson, the word patriotism fell into dispute and disfavor in the earlier half of the eighteenth century. The difficulty with patriot comes with closely related and contrasting words—nationalist, loyalist; flag-waver and jingo (a chauvinistic patriot, or one who supports a belligerent foreign policy).

Individual bravery!

Edith Cavell, the revered British nurse who served in World War I and cared for both friend and foe, said, "I realize that patriotism is not enough. I must have no hatred or bitterness towards anyone." She smuggled Allied troops to the Dutch border during the German occupation and for that she was executed by the Germans.

Now come America and Iraq—weapons of mass destruction and

preemptive strike; domestic politics and foreign policy. Where is patriotism now? Could it be alive in a small Kentucky town? I went looking for signs of it at the Mushroom Festival in Irvine, county seat of Estill.

Patriotism was the theme of the 13th Annual Mountain Mushroom Festival. We thought to ourselves, you know, you could say patriotism is like a mushroom—magnificent when carefully selected and handled just right, pernicious—even poisonous—if misunderstood or taken for granted.

As we sat watching the parade go up the local Broadway, we decided that patriotism could also be compared to a balloon—too much breath and it bursts in your face. A balloon with loose, indifferent handling will escape and confuse best intentions. Deliberately stick a pin in it and any balloon will make a pitiful sound as it goes wiggly, no matter whether it's red, white, or blue.

The midday parade in Irvine was awash with balloons—red, white, blue, green, and yellow. They were not so much symbolic as they were colorful.

Here comes the honor guard. No mistaking the flag or the seriousness of purpose etched in faces, young or old, it didn't matter. Disagreements were postponed.

A New Deal Democrat who said the present occupant of the White House was leading us into economic ruin was respectful when Old Glory waved from the middle of the street.

A woman was asked, "What does patriotism mean to you?"

She replied with a smile, "Love of country...support the troops...support our President."

It was hardly a sampling, much less a poll, but the

203

bright, cloudless sky was a blessing following the cold, early morning rain. There were T-shirts that read, "My cousin is a peacekeeper in Bosnia." Another read: "Be an angel, be an organ transplant donor."

"United We Stand" hats and sweatbands sent their own messages.

The Kentucky National Guard seemed ready, but wasn't spoiling for a fight. A man sold wooden popguns, and that was about as far as weaponry went.

The Shriners were there in force, speaking mainly of helping children's hospitals. The Hillbilly Clan joined in to have a little fun with the stereotypers. The local bookmobile took its rightful place in the parade—Dr. Johnson might've liked that!

Miss Estill County wasn't meandering around with stomach piercings. Instead of talking on a cell phone she was waving to the lines of folks back home on both sides of the street!

Churches had patriotic floats as if to portray the "freedom of religion" part of the First Amendment. Children wore face paintings declaring: "God Bless America."

Someone standing nearby quietly said, "I feel like you ought to help out with your community."

Patriotism—love of and devotion to country—went undefined.

It was alive in Irvine, Kentucky.

Geza

In 1968, Geza Desi became an American citizen. A native of
Hungary, he fled the 1956 Communist invasion of Budapest. He was
only fifteen years old back then, but he knew what he wanted—
freedom.

The idea came to him as naturally as breathing.

"When I made up my mind to leave, I told my father and he said,
'Son, it's your decision. Go, if that's what you want to do and go with
God's blessing.'"

The son never saw his parents again. But, he didn't stop remembering them.

Geza Desi became a refugee to Austria, then Portugal,
then Austria again. Along the way, he was detained
by soldiers, questioned, and released. Finally in
February of 1958, the boy of
seventeen arrived on a plane in New
York. He couldn't speak any English.
He didn't know anybody.

Geza was a determined immigrant
to a New World of promise. "They
pinned a badge on me and gave me
five dollars. They put me on a bus, and

it took me to the train station. They put me on a train, and I arrived in East St. Louis, where I had some relatives."

The Hungarian youth saw a bright future ahead. He intuitively understood the importance of recognizing opportunities and making the most of them. He knew the value of work and sacrifice. He wasn't angry and he didn't blame others. He taught himself to speak English after a teacher told him, "If you're going to be here you're going to have to learn English." Now, at age 59, Geza still has problems writing, but despite a pronounced accent his spoken words and thoughts are crystal clear.

As a young man, he migrated to Wolfe County, Kentucky, right above Sky Ridge, where he worked in a home for children. Three years later he married Wilma, and they realized if they were going to raise a family it was time to earn more money.

Geza moved to Jackson in Breathitt County where he worked as a plumber and air conditioner repairman. He inherited a tradition of sheet metal-working from his father back in Hungary. Repairing pots and pans was an important part of the job, a place to begin.

Next stop: Clark County, where Geza found his home of homes in the community of Ford above the Kentucky River. For the past nineteen years, Geza Desi has been the heating and maintenance man at St. Joseph's Hospital in Lexington. Wilma and Geza's four children have peacefully flourished in their native America: a teacher who is a graduate of Berea College, a tree trimmer, a secretary, and a pharmacy technician.

Ask Geza Desi (he didn't get past the eighth grade) about the Fourth of July, and what you receive is a quiet, gentle lesson about the responsibility that goes with living in a free country.

"First of all, we should think about why we have this holiday. We ought to realize that the Fourth of July was created because people fought for freedom.

"Freedom is something that we all have to work for and appreciate. I was trying to get free. I took a chance at it. Freedom is a commodity that is very precious and, sometimes, we have to give everything we have for that freedom.

Freedom is a hard commodity to pin down.

"The Fourth of July means a lot of people gave their lives for us to have freedom and to have the kind of life we choose to live. Everybody ought to appreciate it. It's more than just a holiday."

Geza Desi is an unusually quiet spoken and mannered individual who doesn't take his country or his freedom for granted. He chooses his thoughts carefully and doesn't rush to be judgmental. In his own words, "We ought to be tolerant of each other."

Truly, it might be said of Geza Desi, every day is his Independence Day.

9/11

In each month of September—on the anniversary of the terrorist attacks on the World Trade Center in New York and the Pentagon in the nation's capital—it's time to speak plainly.

For the past sixteen years the back page of *Kentucky Living* has been a monthly tribute to a kind of daily bread: sense of place and good living based on simple values and freedom from fear without religious dogmatism or authoritarian tyranny.

Longevity with a sense of decency and, certainly, an absence of terror has played no small part in striving for higher meaning. Usually, we stop short of political debate while trying to be sensitive about multicultural creeds and regimes different from our own in the United States of America.

Make no mistake, our national security has come under attack— our sense of individual place has been terrorized, our survival as a nation has been placed in unacceptable peril.

"Nine-eleven" has entered the English language along with "December 7" and "Holocaust." Nine-one-one no longer means just another call for help when an intruder raps on our window in the dead of night, a grease fire has flared in the kitchen and smoke is spreading to our bedrooms, or lightning has struck the stock barn and the horses are wild-eyed, pawing on their stable doors.

Nine-eleven means survival on planet earth.

September 11th is the wedding anniversary of our daughter and son-in-law, Nell and Tim, and it's also the birthday of a neighbor's young son. For them and many more like them whose happy celebrations fall on that date, there'll unceasingly be looks of surprise when asked, "When's your anniversary?" or "When's your birthday?"

"Were you really born/married on September 11th?" For uncounted times they'll say, "Yes, sure was."

In fact, a new awareness was born on that infamous date, or, should have been, because none of us will ever be the same.

What to do?

No time for apathy, no time for weakness, certainly no time for surrender to terrorism. It seems mighty clear that there are those who want us dead—we could renounce all our religious and political beliefs, this enemy would still want us dead.

What to do?

Build our national defense. Sharpen our offense. If we don't, it means we don't believe our institutions are worth defending. More importantly it means we don't believe our individual selves are worth saving.

What to do?

Turn off the entertainment channels long enough to become *informed*. Join the home front by the simple acts of reading, thinking, then *acting* with courage born of September 11, December 7 and the Holocaust.

Jeffrey Goldberg's "The Great Terror," which appeared in the March 2002 issue of *The New Yorker* magazine is journalism at its finest and ought to be read and re-read. It's in-depth reporting that won't be found on anybody's television station.

Goldberg will put readers to considering the likelihood that Iraq's chemical- and biological warfare in Kurdistan was a coldly calculated laboratory experiment in which the Kurds were used as guinea pigs.

Look at the lead picture—the dead man shielding the dead child—and ask yourself, would it make any difference if the doorstep were Kentucky and the victims were neighbors across the street or road?

Thomas L. Friedman's widely praised *From Beirut to Jerusalem*, published in 1989, winner of the National Book Award, serves as a keystone for improved understanding of the Middle East.

Dinesh D'Souza's new book *What's So Great About America* should deflect some of the bashing of America.

As we were working in our little garden here on Plum Lick, we wondered about "nine-eleven" and any other "nine-elevens" to come before our course is run, our life's purpose is finished. We made a promise to ourselves: the innocent victims at the World Trade Center, the Pentagon, and in the plane that crashed in  Pennsylvania deserve our best—and that's what they're going to get.

With our individual sense of duty and our desire to survive as American citizens, we will not yield to terrorism.

Upon Awaking

Too much is happening.

> The snipers.

> Reports from Baghdad. Sliding deeper into Iraq.

> Campaign ads and new varieties of presidential mudslinging.

> Scandal in high and sometimes sacred places.

> Labor disputes.

> Toys dominating holy seasons.

> More violence on television.

> More crude innuendo.

> Just getting up in the morning has its troublesome moments.

> CNN. Global violence.

> Slow down, we say.

> Simplify, simplify, we say.

> It's a possible cure for insanity.

> Take time to smell the flowers before they surrender to another winter.

> Take time for prayer.

> If not prayer, then silence will do.

> If not silence, then a softer tone might help at least for a little while.

The only way we stand a chance to be ready to defend the
  country is to be strong individually.
Gird ourselves with decency and goodness.
Surround ourselves with generosity.
Being mean-spirited won't help.
Road rage won't work.
Perhaps, this is the time for the first really honest conversation
  with ourselves.
Our *best* selves.

Afghanistan

It's a long, twisting path from Plum Lick Creek in Kentucky to the Kabul River in Afghanistan. That is, if you go by boat, then overland. Our little stream of water flows into Boone Creek and winds its way to the Gulf of Mexico—the Kabul River flows to the Indus River and on to the Arabian Sea.

Children know this when they embark aboard their miniature sailboats of common sense.

Kentucky is 40,395 square miles; Afghanistan is 250,775 square miles, more than six times bigger than Kentucky. Another way of looking at it, Afghanistan is larger than the combined land areas of Kentucky, Illinois, Indiana, Ohio, and West Virginia. It's no wonder somebody might stay hidden for a long, long time in Afghanistan.

Kentucky has a population of more than four million; Afghanistan's population is more than eighteen million, more than four times greater than Kentucky and far larger than the combined populations of Kentucky, Indiana, Tennessee, and West Virginia. It's easy to lapse into the misconception that Afghanistan is more or less the size of a postage stamp. Maybe it's because we tend to think that the world map shrinks with distance.

Children know better.

There's a notable connection here, and we'd like to speak to it in the spirit of the Christmas, Hanukkah, and Ramadan seasons.

It's the children.

There are the children of the victims of the World Trade Center massacre, and there are the children running for cover in Afghanistan. There are children of the victims of the Pentagon carnage and in rocky caves there are the children with the barest of life expectancies in the best of times. There are the children who have died and will die with their parents in moments of hideous truth.

What to do?

The Commander in Chief of the United States has guarded answers. The United Nations has resolutions. The maximum leader of global terrorism harbors zealous fanaticism. The Taliban entrenches deeper into unyielding resistance. People gather to pray in churches, mosques, and synagogues. Outside, patriotic songs are sung.

Taunts are shouted.

Hands wring.

Others rise in clinched fists.

Rallies pro and con.

But, the children are born without being skilled in any of these things. They come into the world with an urgent craving to survive. They have an appetite, and they cry for milk, not toys. If they learn greed, it comes later. They long for warmth, especially in times of winter when cold, bitter winds blow down from Canada, Scandinavia, and Turkmenistan.

There are howls of global intrigue, wails of religious conflict, and chills of cultural mistrust. The children want no part of any of it. They've not acquired the alchemist's deceit, the desire to turn base metal into gold or silver. Babies feed at their mothers' breasts and breathe the air upon which no merchant has fastened a price.

It is written in Isaiah:

"A little child shall lead them."

The literal meaning of this doesn't hold up well in a world of advanced technology, but the down-to-earth interpretation seems as clear as it is sound. We grownups inhabiting the globe from Plum Lick in Kentucky to Zebak in Afghanistan owe it to all our children to be as undeceitful as possible, while working to be as strong as we can be. Yes, it's a predicament. But it doesn't mean we have to proceed with adult pigheadedness.

It has been said that freedom is not free. Abraham Lincoln challenged the United States of America to have a new birth of freedom. Winston Churchill said of his beloved land: "Let us therefore brace ourselves to our duty and so bear ourselves that if the British Commonwealth and Empire lasts for a thousand years men will still say, 'This was their finest hour.'"

To this we add from Plum Lick: as we build up our strength, we should never forget the innocence from whence we came.

We are the children. When the children are gone, all is lost. So long as there are children, there is hope.

Hoops

We've come several full circles in our geocentric world, while we here on Plum Lick are reminded of bygone times.

You know, flying a kite, going out and kicking some empty tin cans, skipping rocks across a pond to keep the frogs on their webbed toes—stuff that costs next to nothing.

Don't get us wrong, we're not totally behind the times. We try to stay on a few cutting edges.

Geocaching, for example, is powerfully interesting. It could put us in better touch with geomancy, geochronology and geomagnetic storms.

It's all a part of the learning curve—teaching old dogs some new tricks, keeping our roots well anchored without going to pot.

The wagon wheels with rusty hubs leaning against the above-ground cellar testify as to how far we've come. It's not likely that we'll be using wagon wheels anytime soon, unless it's for support for ivy or flowering mandavilla.

Hardly anything is more un-geoed than the gadget we young squirts used to devise to amuse ourselves when exploring up and down the roads and pathways, back and forth across the unmapped hills of imagination.

Didn't have a name. We might have called it "driving the hoop."

Here's how it operated.

We cut ourselves a five- to six-foot length of #9 fencing wire and went to work. At the business end of the wire, we fashioned a double "U," and at the other end of the wire, we shaped something resembling a handhold. Next we appropriated a hoop from an empty nail barrel.

Nothing fancy.

Just the bare essentials.

That's all it took.

We were ready to roll.

Look out horizon!

The "U" of the end of the wire fitted nicely around the hoop, and we finagled movement. We were in no mood for standing around doing nothing. To be stuck in the mud was as gooey as being up to elbows in axle grease.

It took persistent practice to coordinate the project, which afforded so much inexpensive entertainment—more fun than trying to keep up with a rolling automobile or truck tire. Safer than curling up inside an empty tire and letting some idiot roll another idiot down a steep hill.

After all, the object was to be in control and to keep the movement smooth. The number-nine wire was essential to both considerations. We were going! Little did we think that the day would come when we'd be GEE-oing.

From #9 wire and a barrel hoop, we graduated to our first bicycle, which cost $15.00 and was a beauty. We instinctively knew that the first order of business was to cut a piece of leather and notch it so that it hung nicely over the rear axle. That way, any spilled oil would be wiped clean by the leather and at the same time give the axle a shine

217

that looked like the silver of the gods.

We didn't wear helmets.

But we made sure the chain guard was in place, because the last thing we wanted was to snag and bind our flapping pants legs. When we spun out of control on gravel, we put cool water on our skinned legs, climbed back on the wheels, and continued on our way.

Years passed, geometrically—so it seems.

We won a new bicycle with a radio on the handlebars. The local movie theater (Tom Mix, Gene Autry, Red Rider, Hopalong Cassidy—the good guys), gave the bicycle away after a drawing from coupons earned by exchanging soft drink bottle caps.

We thought we'd died and gone to heaven. Hardly anything could compare with tooling along with soft music playing in the breeze — until it was the year of the first driver's license.

The silly old bicycle with all those musical memories was sent to the junkyard, which turned out to be an almost unforgivable mistake.

Today, with geo-positioning, seat warming, and high-priced, high octane pleasures aplenty, it might not be such a bad idea to take at least one more ride on a non-gas-guzzling bicycle.

We might even find a minute or two for some number-nine wire and a barrel hoop.

Priceless.

Other Hoops

Sitting across the long table at the Whistle Stop Restaurant in Glendale, Kentucky, just south of Elizabethtown, I am struck by one thing: Marianne Walker has written a sparkling jewel of a book.

When Cuba Conquered Kentucky will evoke bittersweet memories for all those who lived through the 1951-1952 "March Madness" when the tiny, proud, and determined farming community of Cuba in southern Graves County was home to the Cubs—Kentucky State High School Basketball Champions.

Marianne Walker was in Glendale to sign her wonderful book, and some of the members of the team that defeated Louisville Manual forty-seven years ago were on hand. Such a time warp! After all, I was only seven years old when Howie Crittenden and Doodle Floyd were making basketball history.

You see, many of us come from these little out-of-the-way farming communities and maybe too few of us dare to dream really big dreams. If you or your children or your children's children want to get a real feel for how that can truly be, whatever you do, pick up a copy of Marianne Walker's *When Cuba Conquered Kentucky*.

Who in the world would have thought that I—a little girl from Woodville, Mississippi—would be sitting down for supper with such handsome Kentucky men as Howie and Doodle?

Pictures of them and their teammates in Marianne's book —Joe Buddy Warren, Raymond McClure, and Jimmy Webb—are stunning to behold: their boyishness; the magic in their eyes; the way they floated through the air; the way they talked the language of the neck of the woods where they were raised up.

The lives and deaths of Cuba's coach, Jack Story, and his sweetheart wife, Mary Lee, are the kind of stories I should like to write. Of course, that would suggest that I have the determination (Coach Story's favorite word) and the research ingenuity of author Marianne Walker.

I would say that she is a good example of a Kentucky woman who's unafraid to tackle tough assignments. She's a professor of English and philosophy at Henderson Community College, and she took a sabbatical to begin the long journey through the lives of young men, their peers, their parents in a crossroads of the Jackson Purchase framed by three major rivers: the Ohio, the Tennessee, and the Mississippi.

You are there in 1951 when Clark County defeated the Cuba Cubs in the championship game for the state title in boys' basketball; and you were there in 1952 when Cuba stormed back to defeat Louisville Manual for the grand trophy. You are there in the motorcade that stretched for fourteen miles from the Eggner's Ferry Bridge to Mayfield, then south to Cuba.

But beyond that, you can be there in the Jackson Purchase before there was rural electricity, before there were paved roads much less interstates. If you want to begin to understand how such a phenomenal thing as the Cuba Cubs could take root and grow, then the first sixty-three pages of the two-hundred and nine-page book are worth the price of admission.

The early chapters include: "Milking, Mowing, Suckerin Tobacco, and Playing Ball," "Dee-troit City Blues," "Death Startles and Stings," and "On the Importance of Acting Right."

Alta Ruth (Howie Crittenden's mother) "worked outside as hard as any man. Every year she planted a large garden and canned many jars of vegetables and fruits, enough to last her family until the next summer. When she was lucky enough to have a cow, she made butter and cheese. She also made most of her family's clothes and quilts by hand."

Lexie (Doodle Floyd's mother) "cooked on the wood-burning stove and baked meals for her large family....She baked biscuits on the lids of five-gallon lard cans. Because her family liked biscuits hot, she'd always have a lid loaded with freshly-made ones ready to pop into the stove. Until the children moved away, the family sat down at the table together for three meals a day. Vodie (Doodle's father) always said the blessing before a morsel was eaten."

When Cuba Conquered Kentucky does not ignore the problem of occasional arrogance born of huge success on a basketball court. My heart goes out to the young teacher who resigned in tears after she was compelled to apologize to the student athletes who had disrupted her class.

It wounds to read and remember gender inequalities in a time when boys are the wonderkinds, girls the barely tolerated cheerleaders and "girlfriends."

But even these troubling thoughts cannot obscure the magic of the Cuba Cubs. In the eighth grade they set a goal, and when they were seniors they reached it.

Coach Story once told his team: "Now you guys listen to me. God gave each of you some ability. You can waste it, or you can perfect it. You perfect it by practicing, and practicing means work."

Coach Story foretold the feat of a courageous man, Lonnie Joe Bowen, who believed in work and walking tall for the less fortunate—all those young people plagued with muscular dystrophy.

Stilts

Lonnie Joe Bowen of Taylorsville comes at you with a big smile that won't quit. In the decade before his three score and ten, he still operates full steam with what could be called a tight triangle of Focus, Flow, and Faith.

Joe's focus is raising money to help fight muscular dystrophy.

His flow is to ride a bicycle across the country to win support for his cause.

His faith tells him he can do it—after all, it was a twenty-years-younger Joe Bowen, who walked on stilts all the way from Los Angeles to Powell County, Kentucky, where he was born in the little community of Bowen, named for one of his ancestors.

The "stiltwalk" required six months to plan (running six miles every day) and six months to plod, one giant step at a time, over a distance of more than three thousand miles in rain and desert heat. Along the way, Joe raised $100,000 for the fight against the disease that each year shortens so many lives in the United States and claims countless victims around the world.

What motivates Joe Bowen?

"I was raised on a farm in eastern Kentucky that didn't even belong to us. At the time, I didn't know that we didn't own it—just rented. As a child and as an adult I have lived the privileged life of a rich man without the burden of having any money. And what a way to go!"

Standing next to Joe in the living room of his elegantly restored home in Taylorsville (Joe Bowen has a special talent for many kinds of craftsmanship), a bicycle waits for its rider.

"It may take me two years to get ready, it may take me four, but I'm going to do it!" says Joe with the positive smile that spreads all over his face, seldom collapsing and turning to a pessimistic frown.

In 1981, Joe wrote a book titled *Stiltwalk*, which traced his journey from Los Angeles to Kentucky: "...I was once more in Kentucky and walking fast. Not in my home county yet, but getting close....Eight miles past Mount Sterling, I walked from Montgomery into Powell County. After crossing the county line, I had about eighteen more miles to walk before I reached the tiny town of Bowen, which had been founded by my great-great grandfather and near which I had been raised on a small farm with my four brothers.

"...Powell County...was never mentioned in the news except when the little Red River overflowed its banks and the valley towns would be nearly washed away. Proud, dependable people lived there—people who worked small farms, raised their children in traditional rural homes, and were concerned about America. I hoped that whatever publicity was given to the walk would somehow help that Appalachian region."

Lonnie Joe Bowen wants to help Appalachia and America, because he and we believe they are inseparable. At the same time, he wants to help the victims of muscular dystrophy.

"I thought about my little friend Robbie Johnson. I could close my eyes and see his smiling face and those big brown eyes—eyes that sparkled when he turned them on you. Would someone find a cure for the disease that had this little boy it its grip?"

The work of MDA, Muscular Dystrophy Association, is as complex as it is costly. With Joe Bowen's smile and positive outlook, a cure for the disease in all its variations one-day will be found. Maybe it will be remembered that once there was a Kentuckian who walked on stilts more than three thousand miles to call attention to the medical challenge before us all.

Later in his unselfish life, when Joe completes his bicycle trip across the country to further the work of the Jaycees, Jerry Lewis, doctors, nurses, and researchers, it'll be remembered, too, that once there was this healthy man from Powell and Spencer Counties, in Kentucky, who did what he could to convince the world that all good things are possible

Mall Walkers

Meet the Mall Walkers.

"I've been walking forever," says perky eighty-five-year-old Bernice of her daily exercise in Lexington's Fayette Mall.

"I've lived across the street since 1972," says Betty, " and I watched the mall being built. We used to walk over here before it became a mall."

The "we" Betty refers to is a group of six to eight ladies who've walked untold miles together.

"When the weather is nice we walk outside," says Betty.

Rising early enough to get to a mall by opening time of around 8:30 a.m., mall walkers all around Kentucky greet one another with friendly "Hellos" and waves as they trek past still-closed shops.

"Any of you seen Santa Claus?" grins one elderly member of the non-threatening opposite sex as he saunters past.

As the walkers make their rounds – four laps equals two miles in this mall, depending on which stores are open—they gradually stop by the food court for a cup of coffee and a bit of conversation with friends.

"You have to make reservations ahead of time," chuckles Orene, whose seat I had mistakenly taken.

"Why do you do all this walking?"

"We do it for the company, mostly," says Bernice. "We all met here at the mall."

"We're a clan, really," Orene chimes in.

More than a clan, many of them consider their fellow walkers as family. "If someone doesn't show up for a day, we call to find out what's wrong," says Orene.

The following Thursday, twenty-five of the walkers were meeting for breakfast at a local restaurant. "We've gone to dinner together, gone on boat rides. We've done lots of things together," says Orene.

"We've had several couples who've met here and married and they still come to walk," smiles Bernice.

Mildred, Bernice, Betty, June, and Orene have an enviable friendship. They've seen one another through various health issues — malignancy, pacemaker implantation, arthritis. Mildred says, before she started walking, she couldn't go very far.

"I couldn't even shop," she says. "I'd have to sit down every few feet."

Now, she walks two miles a day.

Seventy-one-year-old Shirley doesn't take sitting down her necessity for being in a wheelchair. Her feet propel her two miles a day at a pace that would make upright walkers pant. She leans forward with courage and conviction at the same time flexing her fingers for exercise.

The rules of the mall only say, "No running" so they don't keep Shirley from rolling away the aches and pains of her life-long battle with arthritis. No electric motor on this wheelchair – just Shirley power.

On the other hand, or foot, rather, no telling how many shoes this group has worn out. Someone said that they thought about every three years is when shoes need to be replaced.

"I replace my shoes when my legs start to hurt," Mildred reflects.

No doubt about it, they all believe that walking has performed miracles "both mental and physical," says Betty. "There's one man who walks here who has had a heart transplant. Several come and walk with their walkers."

There are mothers pushing their babies in strollers, and men and women of all ages and paces, in singles and in groups. One fellow speeds by doing a walk so fast his flannel shirt's plaid is a blur.

"We walk every day but Saturday and Sunday," Betty says, "and I feel so much better when I walk. I'm so sluggish on Saturday, but I've just got to get some housework done," she laughs.

Any competition?

"We push each other to go that extra mile," says Ken Caudill over his shoulder as he rushes by our table.

Nearby, there is a man who's smiling and listening in. Recovering from a stroke, he also walks, but he uses a rolling walker for his trips. It's outfitted with a purple bicycle horn—just in case someone gets in the way.

Seventy-five miles away in Louisville's Mall St. Matthews, fifty-one-year-old Claudia and forty-seven-year-old Julie get their mall walking done early, too.

"I started walking with my dad thirteen years ago in Wichita. I get my exercise for the day and it makes us feel good," Julie nods toward her walking mate, Claudia.

Claudia and Julie don't pay attention to the mileage. "We walk about a mile and we do that in about twenty minutes."

A young father streaks by, pushing a baby stroller. The child inside is blissfully asleep as the stroller glides over the smooth floor.

"What do you like about walking here," we ask of Julie and Claudia.

"Well, you're not walking in the cold. There's different scenery all the time. It's a lot more fun," they both chime in. "And, it's *free*! You don't have to belong to a gym."

Come to think of it—no wind, no rain and no bitin' dogs.

227

Growing Older

Looking for the best price on gas station signs--$1.99, $2.09, $2.19 — has become a road hazard as dangerous as keying digits — zero through nine — with both hands on cell phone pads while maneuvering through darkening rush hour traffic — four through six — or checking speedometer readings — 35, 45, 55, 65.

We've become the numbers generation.

We're lulled into thinking that $1.99 is significantly different than $2.00 and a $19,999 car is a big bargain when compared to one costing $20,000.

College students fall victim to grade point averages, which suggest that a 2.5 is a lot smarter than a 2.4, and a 4.0 is some kind of guarantee that there's a job out there for five-star bean counters.

Even as it is, the brain has to work overtime remembering bank account numbers, social security numbers, and Uncle Joe's birthday. Why couldn't he have an annual candle-lighting as simple as "I was born" and "one of these times I'll be passing on," and let it go at that?

Aunt Martha doesn't need to be burdened with another "Why, you're as spry as a sixty-year-old...why you don't look a day older than seventy."

Same thing with the price of gasoline. Set a price and leave it alone for a week or two, for Heaven's sake. Pull over, stop, and make the cell phone call. Slow down and leave the speed records to the Indianapolis 500.

People shouldn't be using cell phones while trying to stay out of the way of eighteen-wheelers, and it doesn't seem to make good common sense to try to outwit the pulsating radar apparatus.

Floorboard only when necessary, we say, to get out of the way of something that should be obvious to the 100% law enforcers and the 99.9% law abiders.

Take your average weather forecaster—"thirty percent chance of rain." That means there's a seventy percent chance that the sky's not going to wring out a drop of moisture. "Fifty percent chance of snow." That means a toss of the dime that it's not going to snow.

And then there's that Greenspan fellow with his quarter of a percent prime interest rate. The ups and downs make some of us as nervous as cliff rats.

Back to birthdays!

Since David was seventy-five in February, and Lalie turned sixty on the Ides of March, we decided not to try to surprise each other. We snuggled up to our one hundred and thirty-fifth birthday celebration and let it go at that. No more birthdays. Instead of $2.99 cards we just reached over and gave each other a big old, thousand-percent kiss.

What this means is, numbers be darned! We might have been stitched in the year zero, or we could have threaded the needle in the year 10,000. We is who we is, what we is, when we is, where we is. As for how it happened, we'll settle with the idea that miracles come without price tags, speed limits, or the need to know a precise number on a cell phone so as to call Uncle Joe or Aunt Martha.

We don't count the beating of our hearts when we wake up in the morning, and rush to hook up our arms to the I'm-the-Boss blood pressure machine. We don't try to count the snowflakes on our windshield as we drive down the roads of our unfolding, naturally wintering future. Counting calories and carbs is a poor substitute for moderation.

There's still plenty of time to be on the lookout for another spring and another summer and another autumn, and it doesn't matter a hoot what the number says on the calendar. We're blessed with life, and that's what counts!

The 911 emergency call invention is a good thing to remember, but sometimes it might be better to drop to our knees for more than thirty seconds of prayer.

We might want to listen.

There might be an incoming message of greater importance.

Loretta

A famous man's wife gracefully walked by his side, softly smiled, but took pains to stay out of the limelight.

Just about everybody has known who one-hundred-and-one-year-old Kentucky Historian Emeritus Dr. Thomas D. Clark was, but relatively few have known very much about his wife Loretta.

I decided to sit down with Loretta Gilliam Brock Clark and have a quiet conversation in her home, woman to woman, being respectful of an individual's cherished, well-earned right to privacy.

She was born December 5, 1919, in Lennox, Kentucky, once upon a time a company town in Estill County, a starting place for a long life of memories. Loretta's mother was a schoolteacher and her father was a minister.

She reminded me of my own mother and father, teachers actively involved in the church. I wondered how they would respond to a reporter's sometimes pointed questions. They would have been trusting, I think, the way people were in bygone days before tabloids, paparazzi, and other forms of sensationalism.

The Gilliam family moved to West Irvine and then across the way to Winchester, a time very different from now—before jet streams and interstate highways, before school consolidations and semesters built on convenience.

"Back then, of course, school schedules followed the heat and cold and growing seasons. There was no air conditioning and school started in July back then."

Family was close-knit the way a quilt is patterned. Oh, there might have been an occasional mis-stitch, but the heart of the quilter would be in the right place. Hands were patiently at work as long as there was enough light to see and feel the paths connecting the pieces.

"There were five of us—I'm the oldest—two brothers and two sisters. (Loretta has one brother still living, a retired doctor, thirteen months younger than she.)

The next move was to Lexington, center of commerce and collected knowledge with its own growing pains, then another short move north to Paris in adjoining Bourbon County. The uprootings and replantings had their unsettling moments, but there was never any doubt about the major role played by education.

When it was time for college she commuted to Transylvania University.

"I got up every morning at 5:30 and caught the bus to Lexington."

At the end of her second year, she transferred to Centre College and graduated with a B.A. in mathematics, a field often commandeered by males. Loretta instinctively knew she had a special gift of learning.

"I think math helps because of the discipline and logic."

At the same time, she was generous in her belief that educational precision doesn't necessarily arrive at the same destination.

"For some, a college education isn't for them, but the rewards of a college education are many. I still think that the liberal arts education is the best, preferable to any other. It is very important to understanding."

The Danville community holds a special place in this quiet lady's heart. "Danville was the place where I first got the sense of place—a sense of community," she says with a voice of practiced gentleness.

In Loretta's presence you soon get a feeling of a strong underpinning of Kentucky grit.

"During WWII, I went to California for one year and worked for an extension lab. Before that time, girls stayed in the home. I went out there without a job, but I went with a friend who was also a mathematician and I had a job within a short time. They were so eager to get mathematicians.

"I learned an awful lot. I learned that everybody was marking time, waiting for someone to come back from the war. Everything was suspended.

"I came back and taught math at Irvine High School. The superintendent was wonderful but he ran a tight ship. I came in two months after classes had started—I was twenty-one—and they asked me to teach solid geometry. I'd never had it, but I kept ahead of 'em."

In 1952, Loretta married a young lawyer, Walter Brock, and they said their vows at First Methodist Church in Lexington where her father was the pastor.

Walter and his brother formed the legal firm Brock & Brock. She and Walter had two sons, Walter, now a filmmaker and teacher, and Robert, who is artistic director of Horse Cave Theater.

After Walter's death and the passing of Dr. Thomas Clark's wife, there was one of those unexpected, unplanned turns in the long road awinding.

"I knew his wife Beth and she was a friend of mine—you can have friends and not know their husbands. I had written a history of the Women's Club of Central Kentucky. I found that fascinating, I couldn't put the minutes down—one hundred years of minutes. What women had done was not generally known.

Harriet Van Meter said, "Why don't you call Dr. Clark and ask him to read this?" I said I couldn't, so she did, and he said to bring it by."

"That was in 1996.

"He wrote the preface."

They were married November 27, 1997. He was ninety-two. She was seventy-seven.

"How much of a challenge is it to keep pace with a man as driven as Tom Clark?"

"Every day is so different...if I made one comment on life with Tom Clark—no two days are exactly alike. I'd like to have the housekeepers on the same day every other week, but we always have to negotiate the day due to our schedule."

"Advice to young women concerning marriage?"

"I think it is so important to know yourself. There are some things you just can't give up, it's wise to know that. If there is some dream that you want desperately to follow be sure that the husband you are going to marry knows what that is, will support it, will have the understanding of your fulfilling it. I really am for education. She should have all the education her self calls for, nature calls for, pride calls for, comfort with peers, and society calls for."

"Advice to older women concerning marriage?"

"There have been some second marriages that have been disastrous. After the loss of a husband, a lostness or a loneliness is overwhelming—not acting (on another marriage) in that period—not sharing your life with someone else is a good idea."

"What is your belief about the importance of companionship?"

"If you find it and it's real – take it! If it's real, and if you fall into it naturally, I still believe in some kind of attraction pulling you there. It's a living with someone under all circumstances that requires a deeper feeling.

"It has been a wonderful ride.

"It's extended my life.

"I wouldn't have missed it. He is remarkable, his drive is amazing and it continues every day.

"Days come and days go.

"I love the mountain view of time. The time is life—rhythms are inexorable.

"Today's today and tomorrow's tomorrow.

"Do not argue with the wind.

"There was a time in my life when that didn't fit at all...it does now. Tom will say, 'take it as it comes.'"

Dr. Thomas D. Clark died at 3:45 on the morning of June 28, 2005. On July 14, he would have been one hundred and two years old.

Andy Mead wrote in the *Lexington Herald-Leader*: "For a man whose training was in history, Dr. Clark always lived in the present and thought about the future."

Traveling with David and Eulalie through the woods of Estill County, while doing research about Jesse Stuart and one-room log cabins, Dr. Thomas Dionysius Clark said: "You know, David, if I had another life to live, I don't think I'd give any speeches."

Born in Mississippi, the year of the first Model-A Ford and the flight of the Wright Brothers at Kitty Hawk, Dr. Tom Clark took special delight in referring to his friend, Eulalie, who grew up there, as "Miss-i-sip."

They often laughed about catfish, grits and black-eyed peas.

Eulalie

Mother and Daughter Banquet
Clintonville Christian Church
Clintonville, Kentucky

Thank you for letting me be with you tonight.

It's an honor and a privilege to come here to your church and share this time of sweet fellowship, gathering as we are—mothers and daughters.

I, too, have brought my daughter, Ravy, who is right here next to me.

I'm so grateful to you for asking me to come and be with this precious group of women, women of all ages—because in all of the seventy-five ladies here there are seventy-five very important life stories to be told, and shared, and from which to learn.

For every one of you very young ladies who has come with your mother, there are that many more interesting stories that will be told in years to come. But, for right now, you have asked me to come to share with you some of the things about which I personally feel are important about being a mother.

I suppose I qualify as a mother...I have a daughter of whom I am *very* proud, but I'd like to share with you some thoughts about some women of whom I am very proud to be called their grandchild and daughter.

I was born in New Orleans, the first of three daughters…born to a wonderful young couple, teachers, both of them, who absolutely worshipped the ground each other walked on.

I grew up with two sisters whom I adore today, but at the time we were growing up, my little sister and I were like water and my middle sister poured on the incendiary oil, fanned the flames and gleefully side-stepped it all to sit on the sidelines and grin at the carnage.

My mother loved to tell us stories about her family, and I realize now that the stories were mainly about the women.

At the time, as all young people are wont to do, I really didn't listen as well as I should have, but now I wish I had.

I lost my grandparents before I remember any conversations with them, I also lost my fifty-seven-year-old father just when he and I were becoming really good friends—when I was twenty-eight and by that time I was up and away from where I was raised.

There were remarkable stories of strong, resourceful women, mothers and daughters, who were resilient, adaptable, hard working…with a will to succeed and a determination to do what was right.

There were three things my mother kept pounding into my head at every chance she got which, now I know, came not from her mind, but from her heart and her very genes.

Stand on your own two feet.

Think for yourself.

Do the right thing.

Eulalie Eugenie Gray Harvey, my paternal great-grandmother, the pampered granddaughter of French plantation-owning upper crust in New Orleans, who, in 1884, not only lost her thirty-two-year-old husband but lost everything they had and was reduced to the position of a poetress (not a poet—a janitress—she scrubbed floors) to provide for her two young sons, one of whom was my grandfather.

At her death at the age of forty-six, her coffin was not allowed to be brought up to the altar in St. Louis Cathedral, because she had no money. But, her children didn't suffer because she made sacrifices and was determined to do the right thing, even if it meant getting down on her lily-white knees and scrubbing floors.

God knew what she had done, and so do I.

My maternal great-grandmother, Maria Ann Folds Heaton Bradford, daughter of a Methodist minister, born in Liverpool, England in 1859, boarded a ship right after she was married and came to the United States and headed for St. Louis. When they landed in New Orleans, they were penniless, but they liked the Crescent City so much they stayed.

No grass grew under her feet. While her husband was employed as a window-dresser in one of the Canal Street stores, she used her fine dressmaking talent. Because New Orleans was an international port, all the finest fashions were available for sale up and down Canal Street, but Maria, sketchbook in hand, would stroll from window to window while taking notes about gores and laces, then go home to her shop and reproduce the high priced fashions for a more reasonable price.

In 1890, she had fifteen women working for her and her little daughter, Annie Mary Beatrice, my grandmother, was given a penny a day to pick up the pins on the floor.

Maria was a success in her own business, a pretty remarkable thing for any woman during that time. She and her husband expanded a furniture refinishing business he started to include new furniture, and they were doing pretty well.

Then on January 14, 1910, her husband disappeared. Police

conducted exhaustive searches, but he was never found.

In what must have been a stunning blow to her and her family of eight children, Maria changed horses in midstream, adapted her sense of style in clothes to furniture and accessories and built Bradford's Furniture into one of the largest, classiest furniture businesses in the southeastern United States.

By 1920, she owned the whole block upon which her five-story building was located.

At a time of bereavement, Maria had to think for herself. Far away from her home in England, with no family but her own children, she had to stand on her own two feet.

Even after she was confined to a wheelchair she continued being a strong, revered businesswoman, who educated not only her own children, but also children of lesser means, whom she knew would eventually succeed.

Her daughter, Beatrice, my grandmother, married for love and not money, much to the chagrin of Maria who, against the marriage, gave the new couple no financial help, but Beatrice was found to be made of the same pretty tough stuff her mother was.

She had four children, all eighteen months apart, and she, too, lost her husband at a very early fifty-seven years of age. She, too, had no income from any business or pension.

By using her very limited funds and investing wisely she was able to raise her family on her own. When the Great Depression hit, she had all four of them in Tulane University at the same time.

Audio, the youngest, graduated from engineering school at the ripe old age of sixteen, became a millionaire before he was forty-five and never quit inventing ways for things to work more efficiently and effectively. Cornelius, the eldest, better known as C.B., was a civil engineer and a Lt. Commander in the Navy. He eventually was elected mayor of Key West, Florida. Another of Beatrice's sons, James Henry (Uncle Jimmy), became supervisor of the pressrooms for the Pulitzer Prize-winning New Orleans *Times Picayune* newspaper. He also delighted gatherings of young and old with his magical tricks, adept juggling and infectious laughter.

And then there was her only daughter, Eulalie.

My mother, Eulalie, also married (*with* my grandmother's blessing) for love and not money, and found herself, a big city girl, moving to tiny Woodville, Mississippi (population 1,800), in 1949, with her husband and two small children (eventually to become three) to continue a family grocery business left after the death of her father-in-law (who, by the way, emigrated from Cefalu, Sicily).

An art teacher and Auntie Mame who never let grass grow under her feet, Eulalie, better known in Woodville as "Betty," soon became the linchpin of every civic project that Woodville had to offer, and when it offered none, she invented one to get people involved.

She was constantly thinking ahead, again and again prodding me with those three things:

Stand on your own two feet.

Think for yourself.

Do the right thing.

My father ran the grocery and taught school. She was a teacher also, sporadically because of limitations of the school system. She must have had a premonition that she was going to need something more than that. She wanted something she could call her own. She was seeing the demise of the small grocery as larger, mass markets arrived on the small-town scene.

So, in a small corner of the old grocery, she began a crafts section, which grew a little larger each year.

This was fine, but it wasn't enough.

She incorporated framing and matting materials and pretty soon, she had my father (an industrial education teacher) designing and building machinery for framing and in a matter of ten years, the grocery store that had been Cumbo's Variety Store since 1903 was gone and Cumbo's Frame Shoppe was in its place.

Then, suddenly, my fifty-seven-year-old father was gone. He died leaving my mother with a substantial debt from trying to keep the old grocery afloat and sending his three daughters to college.

What to do?

She did what the women who came before her did—she made sacrifices, but in this instance, cutting corners, literally meant cutting corners.

She stood on her own two feet and with her God-given genes, she worked extremely smart and hard, building a reputation that ranged throughout the southern region of Mississippi and Louisiana.

Her work was stunningly beautiful and her reputation for fine, affordable framing grew.

She paid off the banks by framing items as diverse as full-length admirals' uniforms, lead, cut-crystal walking canes, newspapers printed on wallpaper during the siege of Vicksburg, and turkey feathers and feet (just shot and still juicy—she saved those for me to do!). She framed them all and delighted everyone with her eye for color and talent for superb craftsmanship.

When she finally sold her business in 1994, at age eighty-four, her reputation was such that the buyers of the shop kept the name—Cumbo's.

She had built a tremendously successful business in a matter of nineteen years and many of her clientele never knew she was completely deaf and had been so for over thirty years.

Eulalie read lips, refusing to learn sign language because, she said, "Then, everyone I know would have to learn sign language to communicate with me!"

She was a Wonder Woman to me...she lived by herself and was still getting involved until the end of her life...such as the time she threw a party for a couple, younger than she, who were leaving to move to a retirement center in Baton Rouge.

Who'd she invite?

The whole town!

She put an open invitation in the local paper—just as she did for all her Christmas parties, Easter egg hunts, and anytime her children came home to visit. ANY occasion was an occasion for a party!

My mother, Eulalie, died April 2, 1999. She was eighty-nine years old.

Some of the younger ladies here must be asking, "What does all this mean, anyway?"

Well, it means that there are some women in my family of whom I am very proud, and my daughter, Ravy, and I are fortunate to have some wonderful women to look up to.

I hope that maybe you younger daughters will listen a little closer to your mothers when they share with you those very important stories about your own determined ancestors and what they accomplished against the odds...about what they had to do to:

stand on their own two feet;

to think for themselves;

to do the right thing.

Any of us, all of us, can apply these three things to anything we want to achieve and be a success at whatever we want to do. Sure, there are physical limitations as we get older, but that doesn't mean we can't work around them.

If you want to change your life, change your state of mind.

You have a God-given potential to be the person you have aspired to be...be you nine or one hundred and nine.

You have only one life—don't waste it wallowing in what it presently is or what it might have been.

When we feel good about ourselves, we have more respect for ourselves. Then we have more respect for others. Others, in turn, will respect us.

We have to love our selves first...Not with a haughty attitude, but with the warm, comfortable knowledge inside that we are all very special in the sight of God and that we are all individuals who can make a difference—in our lives, in the lives of others around us, and those to follow.

It will not be without sacrifice along the way, but the sacrifices will be made less painful by the joy of doing something well and something that has made a difference in our lives and the lives of the people we love.

I will leave you with this Victoria Farnsworth quotation I cut out of a newspaper many years ago, right after our daughter, Ravy, was born.

I framed it and sent it to my mother, because I felt it summed up everything I wished I had said to her. Before I sent it, I copied it and it's the first thing I see every day when I sit down to work at my desk.

Not until I became a mother
did I understand how much my mother had sacrificed for me;

not until I became a mother
did I feel how hurt my mother was when I disobeyed;

not until I became a mother
did I know how proud my mother was when I achieved;

not until I became a mother
did I realize how much my mother loves me.

Thank you.

Books

A speech to Bookmobile Librarians, August 2003

Thank you for giving me the opportunity to share a part of this day with you—and for a chance to share a part of me with you—best of all, thank you for an occasion to introduce my wife, the co-author of all I do, Lalie. Without her there would be no *Home Sweet Kentucky* or *Rivers of Kentucky*.

And, I'd like to talk with you a little bit about something else close to my heart.

The year was 1930.

There was a heartbeat.

It was the time of the Great Depression. But there were these people called writers of books, and they worked at their craft no matter how long the bread lines, no matter how many banks closed, no matter how cold the soup.

In 1930, Sinclair Lewis became the first American to win the Nobel Prize for Literature—*Main Street, Babbitt,* and *Elmer Gantry.*

Conrad Aiken's *Selected Poems* won the Pulitzer Prize for poetry. "Preludes to Definition"—human need for self-awareness.

Robert Frost produced his *Collected Poems*, including "The Road Not Taken" and "Mending Wall."

Edna Ferber had a bestseller—*Cimarron. So Big* had already won a Pulitzer Prize and *Show Boat* was rolling on the waters.

Here in Kentucky, a kid from a place called W-Hollow—Jesse Stuart—self-published his first book of poems, *Harvest of Youth.*

After that would come, *Man With A Bull-Tongue Plow, Taps For Private Tussie,* and *The Thread That Runs So True.*

It was a very good year.

It was the year I was born.

And maybe, somehow, it was in my genes, that one day I would become a writer.

Let's go back—not all the way back to 1455 and Gutenberg's invention, the printing press, which would forever change the lives of human beings—but back to the time not so long after the birth year of the United States of America.

The year was 1800—and it too was a very good year. The nation's capital was moved to Washington D.C. Johnny Appleseed was spreading the word. And 1800 was the year that Congress passed a resolution that there ought to be a Library of Congress.

In 1800, there were only fifty libraries in the new nation, and only 80,000 books. Double that many are produced every year today. And—guess what?—it's up to librarians to keep track of them all!

I grew up on a farm here in Kentucky, and by the time I was in school, 1936, first grade, I don't remember being surrounded by books. I'm pretty sure there were few if any bookmobiles.

By the 1940s, we were mainly thinking: basketball and Adolph Rupp—football and Knute Rockne—movies and Gene Autry.

"Have you read the book? No, I'll wait and see the movie."

Then there was high school in a small Kentucky community, North Middletown. The "library" was "study hall," and who wanted to go there? How come all these books are in here? The "librarian" was the unfortunate teacher who had "THE DUTY."

Then there was college: this would be late 40s/early 50s—before computers, so you had the card index file cabinets, row on row, and you took a slip of paper to an unsmiling face at the circulation desk, presented a slip of paper, and waited and waited and waited for the unsmiling face to go into the stacks and bring your book to you. Or maybe word that it wasn't there...so, here's your slip of paper.

The idea of just anybody prowling around in the stacks was unthinkable. An undergraduate might touch a book in the stacks, worse yet, might put the book back in the wrong place! Might turn on the lights! Horrors!

May I tell you about our guiding light—Lalie's and mine? Our basic, fundamental guiding light is our selves, and our own, personal bookmobile. I know you have available these days (if you have the money, and we're talking about a lot of money) you have bookmobiles with "microprocessor climate control systems, double converted power generation systems, local area computer networks, broad-band satellite data links."

That's fine, that's wonderful if you have these.

Lalie and I are what are known as independent publishers. That means we not only write the book, select the paper and the typeface, pay in advance for the book to be printed, promote the book, stand on street corners at festivals and sell the book, and send a chunk of the money right here to Frankfort, where—*maybe*—it is used to add another super modern bookmobile to your fleet.

Or, we give discounts to libraries, and we pay the shipping. We call this subliminal advertising.

We're not embarrassed by the fact that the trunk and the back seat of our car are our shelves for our boxes of books. We're not complaining. We just want you to know that we are in the trenches working for you.

Our 1850 house on Plum Lick is full of books—so full that the house leans to the left, as you look out (toward Frankfort), which is what you would expect from a former CBS News correspondent—Left.

Let me tell you about the stairsteps leading up to the second floor where we write in this old house on Plum Lick. On each step there are books by Kentucky authors: there you'll find Wendell Berry, Robert Penn Warren, James Still, Jesse Stuart, Jim Wayne Miller, Harry Caudill, Gurney Norman, Billy C. Clark, Harriett Arnow, Barbara Kingsolver, Bobbie Ann Mason, Linda DeRosier, Elizabeth Madox Roberts, Harlan Hubbard, Wade Hall, Ed McClanahan, John Ed Pearce, Hollis Summers, John Fox Jr., James Lane Allen, Thomas Merton, Thomas D. Clark, and the newest kids on the block, latest of the Kentucky writers, Chris Holbrook, Silas House, Frank X. Walker, and Crystal Wilkinson. The world could be going to hell in a hand basket, we can be found sitting on one of these steps—reading!—reading the minds of Kentucky writers.

I'd like to tell you about my current project...with Lalie's help. Behind us are *The View from Plum Lick, Peace at the Center, The Quiet Kentuckians, A Conversation with Peter P. Pence, The Scourges of Heaven, Home Sweet Kentucky, Rivers of Kentucky, Follow the Storm: A Long Way Home*.

The newest book we've published is: *Jesse Stuart—The Heritage*, a popular biography, not a scholarly work, but a biography in which I've tried to capture the essence, the soul of a man who seems to be slipping closer to obscurity.

We believe Jesse Stuart (he died in 1984) is cheering you on as you make your rounds in your bookmobiles—maybe they aren't blessed with the latest technological bells and whistles, but they've got four wheels, a tank for fuel, a steering wheel, windshield wipers when it rains—and most important of all—books, books, books.

Some words spoken by Jesse Stuart, who considered himself to be first and foremost a teacher—words from a book titled *To Teach, To Love:*

I'd always liked to see pupils who could make A's in my school, but I came to the conclusion that I would rather have a pupil who made C grades and had A character

247

than one who made A grades and had C character.

In the books that Lalie and I have written about Kentucky and Kentuckians, we've tried very hard to avoid the stereotypes. Jesse Stuart was accused of stereotyping when he wrote *Taps for Private Tussie*. But, the book was biting satire, and maybe it could have been written differently, but that's not for us to say.

We find no satire, no stereotyping in *To Teach, To Love*.

Have you noticed that it is politically incorrect to stereotype just about anybody except the people of Appalachia, especially eastern Kentucky?

Here are some words from one of our books, *Peace at the Center*, the words of the late Gov. Bert Combs, as told to us by his widow Sara, presently chief judge of the Kentucky Court of Appeals.

> *He used to always say that he never wanted to hear young people from Eastern Kentucky apologize for being from Eastern Kentucky—that they could do anything—that the key to it was education, they could go anywhere in this country and do anything...I used to give him some quotations that he used in some of his speeches— especially during school reform. 'After bread, education is the first need of the people...There was another one, a Chinese proverb, that he used a lot...'If you're planning for a year, sow rice. If you're planning for a decade, plant trees. If you're planning for a lifetime, educate a child.'*

And this is where you come in—librarians and drivers of bookmobiles. You've come a long way since 1953, when there were ten bookmobiles in operation in Kentucky. The following year, the group called "Friends to the Governor" brought eighty-four more bookmobiles to the State Fair, and Gov. Wetherby presented them to the counties.

Working together with a sense of community, we are making a difference and we congratulate you for your commitment to the idea of books.

Cedar Shavings of Time

If we're not careful we might conclude we just arrived here on earth unrelated to thousands of others much braver and likely just as interesting as ourselves. We might not even give a whittler's dern about all those who've gone before us.

We might never know how it must have felt to have flatboated or steamboated down the Ohio, canoed up the Missouri, and slogged the rest of the way up the Platte toward Oregon in 1866, only twenty years after the British relinquished their claim to the Oregon Territory.

It's one thing to have read Francis Parkman's *Oregon Trail,* Kentuckian A.B. Guthrie Jr.'s *The Way West,* or James A. Michener's *Centennial.* It's another important piece of business to know that maybe just one restless, reckless, or feckless cousin or a whole passel of kinfolks felt passionate about extending the United States of America all the way to the Pacific Ocean.

The idea of Manifest Destiny has been denounced for as much malevolence as it has been praised for benevolence, but that's a debate best left to historians, humanitarians, and roving evangelists.

The issue at hand is to put out a bugle call to discover who we are and who we were, where we are, where we were, and who we might become. It's basic genealogy, the study of family connections—good or bad, right or wrong.

I had thought all along that my grandfather, Rev. Coleman W. Dick, was an only child. Nobody in our family ever said a word about even the possibility of other brothers and sisters, the children of Van and Zerelda Stephens Dick. (She's buried in Cave Hill Cemetery in Louisville, but we don't know where great-grandfather Van was laid to rest.)

After giving a talk at the historical and genealogical society in Salem, Indiana, I happened to mention the names of Van and Zerelda. About two years later, after one person had spoken to another person and that individual had passed along the names of my ancestors to somebody else, did I discover that a child of the Dick family left what would come to be known as Kentuckiana and headed for Oregon!

The source of my new knowledge is Edmund G. Fisher's *Descendants of Thomas and Jane (Jefferson) Stephens of Baltimore County, Maryland, 1745-1999*. Cousin Ed, the genealogist, and we now talk by e-mail between Kentucky and Oregon, and we now know that Van and Zerelda (Ed spells it Zerilda) had ten children: Philip, Franklin, Mary Elizabeth, Harriet, Silas, Martha, Samuel, Joseph, Coleman (my grandfather), and Sarah.

Frank became postmaster at La Grande, Oregon, and later was elected to Oregon's House of Representatives (1885-1888) and Senate (1888-1891).

"For some thirty-five years the Dicks made their home in a large, though not particularly distinctive, Victorian mansion at S.W. 14th and Salmon Streets, in Portland's central business district. This home was demolished long after Frank and [his wife] Marquis' deaths to make room for a freeway expansion project."

When I was in Portland for a twentieth century educators' conference I didn't know that one of my ancestors one hundred years before had walked the same downtown streets. And, Oldham County, Kentucky, will never be the same, because "Rilda" and Van's roots are there: "As newlyweds, the Dicks lived briefly near Madison, Indiana, but by 1838 were residing on a two hundred and thirty-acre farm at Westport, Oldham County, Kentucky, where Van had strong family ties. Ohio River trade dominated Westport's commercial life and provided ample business for the small cooperage Van operated for some years on his farm. The couple's ten children were born and reared in Westport. Little of Van and Rilda's later lives is currently known."

This is where I do my genealogical part. The next edition of Cousin Ed's mammoth volume will include the descendants of grandfather Coleman, my father, Samuel, my daughter, Nell, and her daughter, Celina Rose, who has the distinction of being the first descendant of Thomas and Jane Stephens to be born in the twenty-first century.

It becomes the challenge and the joy of Celina Rose to take the first steps toward another new century. May she be guided by the best arising within her own state of mind. May her children and her grandchildren savor the essence of the preceding generations, then map their own way to their truest destinations.

Mother's Day

On this Mother's Day, my mother would have been one hundred and three years old. The picture hanging above our fireplace was taken when she was sixteen. She had long locks of hair, and there was an angelic expression in her eyes. She probably dreamed of having lots of happiness.

I wonder now how I might honor her, because, you see, my mother had a hard life, and I believe she deserved a whole lot more than she ever got. Her runaway teenage marriage to my father, a gifted young physician and surgeon, ended with his death at the age of only thirty-six.

Lucile Barnes Crouch Dick loaded up my two older sisters and infant son into a Model-A Ford, and we returned home to Kentucky. It must have been a long and bitter ride from Cincinnati, down old U.S. 27 through Falmouth, Cynthiana, and Paris, to North Middletown. I was too young to remember. I just expected to be fed and have my diapers changed. If there wasn't a little something on my birthday, that would be all right, because we didn't have any money, and I was just as happy with nothing at all.

Poor as clabber milk.

When I was four years old, my mother remarried. We moved out to a big farm called Mt. Auburn, and by the time I was ten I'd learned about hitching up a team of horses and going out to bring in a load of corn. I saved pennies and rolled them tightly. Dimes and quarters were as dear as five-dollar bills. I went to school and behaved myself. I valued my teachers and avoided trouble.

Lucile's second marriage lasted ten years and ended in divorce. It's not any furriner's business to know the reasons.

Now, Lucile and both her husbands sleep in the North Middletown Cemetery, where one day Lalie and I will join them. While we used to dread that thought, we look at it differently at age seventy-five and sixty, respectfully—more positively, we mean to say.

What has happened?

Five years ago, I was named Chairman of the Board of the North Middletown Cemetery. There are seven members of the board, and they do everything they can to show respect for all the mothers and fathers who've gone before.

When graves are dug, one of us is there to try to be sure it's done properly. We set out the chairs beneath the tent and wait for the arrival of the hearse and the funeral party. When "Amazing Grace" is sung, we sing too. When there's a prayer, we close our eyes and bow our heads. When the service is ended, we wait our turn to go to the young man who has lost his mother, and we say, "I'm sorry."

After the family has left, we help move the casket to the grave, and we are present for the interment. We carry the flowers and place them on the fresh-turned earth. We fold up the chairs and return them to shelter.

I know this sounds sad, maybe something you'd just as soon not read about. But, we believe you can judge a community by how it cares for its cemetery, especially a small place by the side of the road, or up on a hill in a forgotten country graveyard.

At the same time, this brings us to another thought. I believe you can pretty much take stock of a person's quality by how he or she respects Mother while she's living. Maybe she's weary with worrying about you. She might be more contrary than ever before. But even if she's forever nagging, it probably doesn't hold a candle to how demanding you were when you depended on her for your very life.

She may be around the corner or just over the county line, or she may be struggling for breath in a nursing home or in hospice. Wherever she is, she deserves some flowers on this Mother's Day and, maybe, a prayer or two would be appreciated.

Father's Day

I've often wondered about the father I never knew.

He died when I was eighteen-months old.

Samuel Stephens Dick died in the depths of the Great Depression, 1931, the year of Pearl buck's *The Good Earth*, six years after Theodore Dreiser's *An American Tragedy*—a bracket of time symbolizing loss of innocence and sense of place and the failure of Jazz Age excesses.

Bread lines.

Prohibition.

Medical school laboratory gin.

Dr. Samuel Stephens Dick didn't practice long enough to leave a lasting reputation or a legacy. His too-early death during the Great Depression—that single American tragedy should have taught us to beware of mind-altering gratification. We should remember to take care of ourselves while taking care of others.

We were told, Sam had a marvelous singing voice, and although I don't remember hearing it, I choose to believe he leaned down close to my face at nighttime and sang me to sleep. I'll bet he did that more than once. He was a tenor.

They said, Sam wanted a son so that he could give him the name of his best friend, David Barrow, the son of Dr. David Barrow of

Lexington, Kentucky. The elder David led the Barrow Medical Unit in World War I, but young David drowned in Lake Michigan, and my teenage father was one of the grieving pallbearers.

Another American tragedy.

So, here I am with all these memories whispering in my seventy-five-year-old mind, and each year, when Father's Day rolls around, I think how fortunate anybody is who has had a loving father for just one shining moment.

In the mail has come a warm letter, which I'd like to share as a way of honoring dads throughout Kentucky on Father's Day. The writer is Michael Wallace from Paint Lick in Madison County. Mike has his own remodeling and repair business, and he and his wife have three sons.

Michael writes:

You have praised the character of the people of Kentucky. I'm enclosing a writing about an outstanding man: Daniel Eugene Wallace, pipe fitter, farmer, friend, my Dad.

He lived from September 2, 1933 to January 30, 2001. A lifetime Lawrence County Kentucky man, on the banks of the Big Sandy River, he lived.

Here's a portion of Michael's letter, which originally appeared in *The Big Sandy News.*

Thank you, Dad...

For your sense of humor, for singing in the Church choir, for laughing at yourself, for working and playing

256

*hard, for hunting with me, for our talks in the garden, for
my first car, for the countless twenty-dollar bills you
handed me, for treating Mom like a lady, for making us
hoe the corn, for being a dreamer, for raising us in Church
and Sunday School, for our silage days on the dairy farm,
for all the early morning trot line runs, for playing with us
when we were little boys. I love you.*

Thank you, Dad...

*For marrying Mom, for helping us go to college, for the
years of batting practice, for dressing up at Halloween, for
the time we picked blackberries under a full moon, for the
many times you co-signed for us, for telling us stories in
bed, for teaching us how to pray, for the calves and chicks
and kittens and puppies and pigs and ponies, for
memorizing and quoting Scripture, for marrying Mom.
Yes, I've said it before and again, thanks for marrying
Mom.*

I love you.

We don't all have the good fortune to have a father like Daniel, who lived sixty-seven years. Those of us who've lost our fathers before the age of remembrance and those who've been neglected or had abusive paternal experiences will come to terms with our own realities.

Yesterday is gone and what is past is past. Tomorrow isn't here yet, so we can't do anything about that until it's here. What matters most of all is now.

The challenge is to be the best father we can possibly be to our own children, and pray that our sons and daughters will honor us by the way they relate to the next generation...and that will become the better Kentucky future which will be the gift to the generations that follow.

Nature Preserve

We hereby resolve to visit at least six Kentucky State Nature Preserves during the year 2006. This will leave six for 2007 and another six for 2008, and we'll still not be finished.

Kentucky presently has forty-four State Nature Preserves, and there's probably one close to where everybody lives.

This idea of caring and walking the walk came to us after we discovered the Jesse Stuart State Nature Preserve in Greenup County. It includes seven-hundred and fourteen acres and there are protected trails to gladden and maybe strengthen most hearts

We drove over to Frankfort, located the Kentucky State Nature Preserves Commission office, at 801 Schenkel Lane, and introduced ourselves to the folks who know the many differences among wildflowers, fish, and wild animals—and their inalienable right to live as close to nature as the Great Creator intended.

Here are some suggestions from the Directory of Kentucky State Nature Preserves, about where to go and what to expect:

The Blanton Forest SNP—More than three thousand acres in Harlan County with trees as much as three to four feet in diameter, as high as one hundred feet tall—oaks, hemlocks, and many other kinds of "canopy" trees. Watch out for the snakes and remember, they are protected too!

John B. Stephenson Memorial Forest SNP—A one hundred and twenty-four-acre wooded gorge with two waterfalls in Rockcastle County, this preserve honors the memory of the former President of Berea College. Anglin Falls and Venable Falls are there for the viewing. Be careful about the slippery rocks!

The Tom Dorman SNP (formerly the Kentucky River Authority Palisades SNP and renamed in honor of the former director and commission chairman of the Kentucky River Authority) is only accessible from the Garrard County side of the Kentucky River. Beware of extremely high cliffs. The views from boats are breathtaking.

The Goodrum Cave SNP, located in Allen County is the Commission's first purchase of a cave for the protection of an endangered bat species. Access is by written permission only. This site protects a maternity colony for thirteen thousand gray myotis bats, listed by the SNP Commission as one of three federally endangered bats found in Kentucky.

The late Dr. Mary Wharton of Georgetown College established Floracliff SNP, located on the Kentucky River in Fayette County. "Below Elk Lick Falls is a tufa formation, which resembles a frozen waterfall." Visitation is by appointment only and is restricted to small groups led by approved leaders.

So, this might represent the first six preserves to visit, the second set might include: Crooked Creek Barrens SNP in Lewis County; Lower Howard's Creek Heritage Park and SNP in Clark County; Three Ponds SNP and Obion Creek SNP in Hickman County (written permission only for both sites, and in the same area is the Kentucky portion of Reelfoot National Wildlife Refuge in Fulton County; Kingdom Come State Park Nature Preserve is in Letcher County (strict rules of access due to the federally endangered Indiana bat); and then the trip we've been saving up for—Bad Branch State Nature Preserve in Letcher County. This preserve contains Bad Branch

Gorge, "A forested gorge on the south face of Pine Mountain...one of the most significant and beautiful natural areas in the state."

After we've done all this during the next two years, we're still not half-way finished! So many miles to go, so many trails to hike, so many sunrises and sunsets to witness, so many pictures to take with our own mind's eye.

No need for a passport, no clearing customs and immigration, no standing in line at ticket counters and currency exchange windows.

For the life of us, we can't imagine forking over perfectly good money for a Caribbean cruise or a grand tour of Europe—at least until we've run out of things to enjoy here so close to home.

Lampus Wood

There we were at Renfro Valley in Rockcastle County, Kentucky, minding whittling and such, when a gentleman from Tennessee moseys up and asks us to take ahold of his walking stick.

Detecting by the tenor of his twang, we judged the stick would probably be substantial, something you could use sharply on a snake or snapping dog.

To our surprise, the stick was nearly as light as a gaggle of goose feathers.

"Lampus wood," says the gentleman. "Grows only around my place, just over the line in Tennessee."

"Nowhere else?"

"Nowhere else!" he says, going ahead full gainer.

Well, he had us. You can't argue nearly as nicely when somebody gives you something. He presented us with two lampus wood walking sticks. Along the length of them, there are natural markings where the sprouts once hung. Stripped of these, the markings look like Indian flints. At the top of the stick you can see a soft core running straight through to the other end.

"I'm Howard Branham of Hilham, Tennessee," says the gentleman who, when he says "Come visit," really means it.

Hilham crossroads is in Overton County due south of Standing

Stone State Park and Forest in a valley to the south of Good Pasture and Wilson Mountains—all of that across the line in the Volunteer State. Mr. Branham is waiting, true to his word. He shows us to chairs around the wood stove sitting on "Tennessee sandstone right out of a quarry nearby...my wife Johnie mortared every stone." The stove is fired with split hickory.

The conversation moves to whittling. David takes out his Hen and Rooster, which Mr. Branham admires with courteous circumspection. He opens a toolbox, takes out a little pad of carbon steel, and removes a burr from one of his Kentucky brother's blades. He takes the cutting edge at an eight- to twelve-degree angle and makes ten strokes in each direction on a well-worn whetstone.

"What's the difference between a Kentuckian and a Tennessean?" we venture.

"A Kentuckian is a Tennessean with his brains knocked out," replies Mr. Branham, smiling.

We recall what Irving S. Cobb once said:

"The Tennesseean is more a Southerner than he is a Tennesseean, the Kentuckian is more a Kentuckian than he is a Southerner—more a Kentuckian, indeed, than he is anything else whatsoever. From center to circumference, from crupper to hame, from pit to dome, he's all Kentuckian."

Maybe Mr. Cobb is correct, but as for Mr. Branham, he's just a retired truck driver who spent several years in Deetroit City. He was born between Little and Big Renox Creeks in Kentucky.

"I was born in a little three-room cabin. The day I was born, the snow blew through the cracks in the wall and piled up inside. My grandmother midwifed me. Dad farmed all his life...couldn't read or write...couldn't count...Mother made it through fourth grade...I was first in the family to graduate from high school...walked to school...born in '32."

Mr. Branham shows us his thicket of lampus trees, which he says may be related to the sumac family. He explains the possibility of using sections of the miniature trunk as popguns. Mrs. Branham remembers lampus as the "chewing gum" tree.

Mr. Branham lays out most of his knife collection—Copperhead, Fighting Rooster, Granddaddy Barlow—thirty to forty knives. He's a supporter of the National Knife Collectors Association located in Chattanooga.

"Go to bed early, get up early...triple bypass, hip replacement...walk two and three-quarters miles every day...whittle every week...set my chair on piece of sheet, put my feet on this fireplace rock, and make a mess. Cedar's the only thing any good."

A fluffy pile of cedar shavings is what we see when Mr. Branham takes us up to Claude Lee's Service station at Hilham crossroads, unincorporated. Mr. Lee, a tall and spry seventy-five-year-old, has been nineteen years on one corner, seventeen years on the other.

"He can do it all," says one of several whittlers of cedar.

Claude Lee is grateful that for more than thirty years he's "been making a living." He specializes on "tires and brakes" along with a generous amount of whittling cedar. He presents a cedar rolling pin to Lalie, and they laugh about the likelihood that she might hit her husband over the head. She holds it out, squints, and indicates she'll probably stick with biscuit dough.

"You O.K.?" says Mr. Lee to a gas customer who has come in with his money.

"Why, yeah, fine as a fiddle."

"Don't want to live in a bigger town," echoes a voice from the vicinity of the cedar shavings.

"When you're a loafer, you have to wait on the front," says a resting whittler, handing greenbacks to Mr. Lee.

"We use the pile of cedar shavings to get the fire started."

Mr. Branham wants us to meet ninety-five-year-old Emily Maxwell, who lives nearby. This morning, she's baked several folded-over fried-in-lard pies. She doesn't own a television set, says she doesn't want one. Listens to a little radio, reads magazines—"Do my Bible lessons...raise a garden every year."

Her prescription for a long life? "Hard work...stay away from doctors...try to stay well."

Mrs. Maxwell was a real Rosie the Riveter in World War II. She worked in the blimp department of a factory in Akron, Ohio, but in due time she returned to her birthplace in Overton County, Tennessee. She wanted to help take care of her aging father, who lived to be ninety-two. Emily waited until mid-life to get married. "I reckon I was so mean nobody would have me," she says with a sparkle in her eye. She married mule trader and blacksmith, Burr Maxwell, and until the day he died they lived in this same little house by the side of the road. His shop, built with hand-hewn tulip poplar logs, still stands by the well house cellar. "Everthing is just like it was the day he died," says Emily, giving us permission to go see—grindstone, blower, sharpeners, wheels, hand tools, and gadgets aplenty.

Emily lives in the present time of bachelor's buttons. "You ought to have seen them about a month ago," she beams. The conversation turns to zinnias, beans, corn, tomatoes, melons, squash, and cucumbers. Her handmade quilts and afghans grace sofa and chairs, and we choose not to speak of anthrax or Afghanistan.

"Will you raise a garden next year?" we ask.

"I hope," Miss Emily replies.

In 2005, she turned ninety-nine and when Howard Branham showed up in spring to work up her garden, he said, "You sit here on the porch and I'll do it."

She said, she'd help all she could, because when the time comes for Miss Emily "to go," she says she wants to be working in the garden.

David and Lalie travel home to Plum Lick with the comforting reassurance that the Kentucky state of mind can begin here and settle richly shared in Tennessee or anyplace else on planet Earth.

Museum of Appalachia

We head south on Interstate 75, skirt Jellico, and trace the western edge of Pine Mountain. The parallelogram of Tennessee seems more spacious in the sweep of Appalachia stretching down from the tight triangles of eastern Kentucky hollers.

Maybe, it's a case of a peek over the state line being greener on the other side—flowers sweeter, rivers grander...Clinch, Holston, and French Broad.

The drive from Jellico cuts southeast across Little Cumberland Mountain, over Cumberland Mountain, alongside Cross Mountain, Walden Ridge, and Pine Ridge. We've called ahead to Glenn Greene on the edge of Knoxville, and we've agreed to meet at the Museum of Appalachia on Buffalo Creek in the valley of Lone Mountain.

Passing through the museum entrance gate is occasion to shed franchised thinking and to put on simpler garments of long ago. Shoes don't need to be shined, pants don't need to be pressed, horns don't need to be trumpeted, road rage is especially out of place.

Millstones tell us this.

Poled haystacks speak to it.

Sheep nibble.

Chickens scratch.

Male peacocks preen.

"What's the difference between a violin and a fiddle?" we joke at lunch with Glenn Greene, master craftsman of musical instruments.

"A violin has strings. A fiddle has strangs," we agree, and we smile with the softest of laughter. "And the violin costs about six thousand dollars more," we rejoice.

Glenn, whom we first met at the "Mountain Masters" in Harlan, Kentucky, is an extraordinary spirit of gently-proclaimed Appalachian soul. We're especially fascinated by the nyckelharpa, with musical roots in the thirteenth century of Sweden, a non-feuding relative of the hurdy-gurdy, not to be confused with the noisy barrel organ. To build one from scratch requires deep patience and exacting handiwork.

The nyclelharpa has more frets than a musician has fingers, and one of Glenn's favorite "happies" is to tell a new acquaintance how he once ordered two more fingers, but the manufacturer only sent him one. Whereupon, Glenn removes the lid of a small case and inside is one finger (which he has poked through a hole in the bottom).

Again, the shy chortle and the sparkle in the eye.

Glenn also has an assortment of pencils in his shirt pocket all lined up as if they are the same. When he pulls them out one at a time: the first is very short for poems and short stories; the next is very long for books; one has points on both ends for those times when he is free of mistakes; one has erasers on both ends when he can't seem to do anything right.

We walk past the tulip poplar trunks made into long benches for the festival crowds when they enter through the small gate in the split rail fence to the cabin where the sign reads: "Come upon the porch and sit awhile."

We take our places with guitarist Ted Wyrick, mandolin player

Tony Thomas, and banjo player Linda Gunderson. There's a polite pause as Glenn Greene uncases his nyckelharpa, and the next thing you know we're into "There's Appalachia, Can You Hear It?" Tony Thomas vocalizes it, and we're refreshed by it.

Go on, stretch out your legs.

Readjust your panty hose.

Loosen your stupid tie.

Regard your brogans, which you had the better sense to wear. Entwine your non-musical fingers behind your knotty head. Breathe the cool breezes.

Smile.

Let go.

"There's a black top through the holler where the hog path used to be," sings Tony, and we accept the inevitability of Interstate 75 and all its macadamized connections. But, there's no law that says we can't get off of it every once in a while, walk up to a cabin porch, and lose ourselves in memory.

Today, the audience is small—a couple from Wyoming, another from Michigan, another from Pennsylvania, and we Plum Lickers from Kentucky. In between the songs evolve the stories told by each one of us as we seem moved to oral history.

We tell about the time when our pickup truck, Old Blue, refused to go forward and would only move in reverse. We tell how we drove it that way on the farm for a season no matter what the neighbors might be thinking. We explain how all trips had to be carefully planned, because there would be those situations from which there might be no return (an edge of a steep drop-off for instance). One of the best parts about driving backwards, though, we sagely observe, is that you have an excellent view of where you've been.

David and Lalie, traveling companions through Appalachia, join in with what happened when we finally took Old Blue in for a transmission fix. Lalie had followed David home after the repairs, and what she saw was the result of hauling too many sheep to market. Cornstalks were tall and tasseling out, sight to behold as we headed down the road.

"There's Appalachia can you hear it?" sings Tony, "There's Appalachia can you leave it?" the words so blended with Ted's guitar, Linda's banjo, and Glenn's nyckelharpa.

We can see it, and we can hear it, and we don't want to leave it. We'll be here in the fall for the annual homecoming.

Twilight

As we looked westward from the hillside above Plum Lick Creek on the last month of the twentieth century, we wondered about this "last" business, this thing about ringing down history-making curtains.

Closure is a cleansing idea, but staying alive is a song giving feet something to dance about.

> *All the world's a stage,*
> *And all the men and women merely players:*
> *They have their exits and their entrances…*

Yes, dear Shakespeare, but there has to be more than this, more than your "seven ages." If there is no hope, then we surely must create it from within our own God-given imaginations.

> *Life is real! Life is earnest!*
> *And the grave is not its goal;*
> *Dust thou art, to dust returnest*
> *Was not spoken of the soul.*

Thank you, mellow Longfellow, worthy companion as we step carefully along the creek banks of immortality. To be sad, to be gloomy, to be fearful, heavy-hearted and forlorn is to ignore the simple song of the birds in our water maples.

Listen! The mighty Being is awake,
And doth with his eternal motion make
A sound like thunder—everlastingly.

Ah, Wordsworth, gentle friend, help us to save and savor this December of our lives and come with us into the new millennium of all we yearn for.

In the October of our autumn, we moderated a community forum: *Kentucky General Assembly 2000: Legislation for Seniors in Kentucky.*

Yes, we talked about retirees by the bushelful, whether or not to dip into the social security fund, the high percentage of us that will spend our last days in nursing homes, prescription drug issues, slot machines, and video lottery terminals.

What to do?

The next morning we turned to Shakespeare, Longfellow, and Wordsworth, but then more importantly turned to our selves of selves.

Did we pray?

Yes, we did.

But we did not go pleading for quick, easy fixes. In the last month of the last year of the twentieth century (Gregorian calendar— Christians should acknowledge the presence of the Jewish and Moslem calendars) we're warming up for new possibilities, new parts to play.

When was the last time we really visited a nursing home? Did more than walk in, check the room number, go to the person of yesteryear, and say more than, "Hello. How are you? I'm fine. Wish I could stay longer. Have to go. See you next time."

When was the last time we made an appointment to sit down with our elected legislator (Frankfort would be a good place to begin) and spent fifteen minutes explaining how important we believe it is to fund just one of the AARP's *Kentucky Legislative Goals*? the "Kentucky Health Insurance reform statute?" the "protection of consumers from abuse and fraudulent practices?"

Each day, each one of us is another day older. But that doesn't mean we have to be increasingly uncaring, indifferent to the plights of others, remorseful about our own late hour.

Recently, we were introduced to a woman who in the month of December, in no winter of any discontent, was ninety-four years old. She had just returned from a trip to Iceland (which she said was not as much fun as Antarctica), and she said she was leaving soon for a boat trip up the Snake River (1,038 miles long with a canyon more than forty miles long and 7,000 feet deep)!

On the night we saw her, she smiled as she walked out onto the dance floor with confidence that would have made John Travolta's heart pound.

As for ourselves, we've written here from our heart for this new century, recalling the words of many pilgrims, including Alfred, Lord Tennyson:

> *Come my friends*
> *'Tis not too late to seek a newer world.*
> *Push off, and sitting well in order smite*
> *The sounding furrows…*

Autumn

As the water maple leaves piled up around our house we resisted the temptation to rake them and bag them and tote them down the lane for the garbage truck to swallow up and spew out into a landfill someplace.

First of all, we're not sure that trying to bring artificial order to the spectacular chaos of autumn foliage makes any sense whatsoever. Secondly, we're opposed to overuse of plastic bags, because it's just one more container to have to throw away and be buried. Thirdly, the whole idea of institutionalized garbage collection in rural areas is questionable at best, because it increases the temptation to ignore our own consumption messes.

Actually, we support universal, mechanized, public garbage collection, because we can see most of our rural areas becoming increasingly urbanized.

The Rural Kentuckian has understandably become *Kentucky Living*, for example. Our problem has to do with the phenomenon of leafage, and it is to that end that we would like to exchange some ideas with all lovers of the autumn season.

The falling of leaves, of course, is a natural scattering, and the benefits include the loaming of the land. Layer upon layer of generational leaves have left us a rich humus within which civilizations have found their roots. While it may be true that too many fallen leaves acidify the soil to troublesome levels, and while it may be psychologically important to go out and furiously rake leaves once a year, there's something else worth considering—taking the time to watch the leaves falling from the water maples is good for the soul. The idea is to be a participant in the changing of the season, rather than simply as spectator. Some folks aren't pleased at all until they've driven all the way to New Hampshire or Vermont to watch the foliage spectacular.

As a child growing up on a farm in Kentucky, the last thing in the world we'd think about doing would be to take a long, expensive trip to see leaves changing colors someplace else. It would never have occurred to us to buy a camera and load it with film B.D. (before digitalization)—to document what we'd seen. We'd stay at home and use the cameras of our minds, our beings, and our innermost satisfactions to know and hold intimately the autumnal experience.

As another leaf unloosens its bond to the tree, and as it floats earthward, we turn to each other and say, "I love you," and "Do you remember the time...?" and "Look over there, do you see what I see?"

This is no time for the crunching of piles of leaves into plastic bags. This is the time for understanding the miracle of autumn becoming winter, and in due time to become spring again with the return of fresh, new leaves.

We are leaves, are we not?

Are we not leaves, more that we are trees?

Or, in another way of thinking about this, leaves are trees, and trees are leaves.

The likeness of humankind and the families of leaves are a pleasant and satisfying contemplation. We begin our lives with the exuberance of springtime. When we are forced from our sleep within the buds borne of generations of trees.

In summer, combinations of sunlight, water, and microorganisms interact to produce food for the trees of life, while at the same time expanding the volume of life-giving oxygen for a thirsty atmosphere.

It works magically, doesn't it?

The process of photosynthesis, or the manufacturing of food, is akin to a body, whose various parts should be working in harmony. The result is not only survival, but also the enrichment of all living things.

Eternal spring and summer are contrary to our way of life in Kentucky. Autumn and winter are necessary to complete the seasons that make us unique. If we can only come to understand that what we are has depended so greatly on all those who've gone before us, and what we do now and in the future will matter immeasurably to those who follow after us.

As we sit here, you and I, watching all these glorious water maple leaves descending, we know what our destiny is. We give grateful thanks to those who are sleeping in the earth, and we take solace in the knowledge that our own descendants resting in tomorrow's dreams may one day recall that we were intimately involved in creation.

Letters

From time to time there's a connection that makes all the whittling of words worthwhile.

It comes in a letter from Debra Salsman of LaRue County. Her husband passed away last November. It had been a long journey of poor health, but she remembers him for his love of family, people — and knives.

"He needed a way to remain connected to people. His life-long fascination with pocketknives, Case knives in particular, gave him exactly what he needed.

"He and a friend, who was also retired, traveled Kentucky, finding flea markets, knife shows, and knife clubs. There were London and Greenville, Leitchfield and Louisville, Cave City, Glasgow, and Halifax. At all these stops, he found knives to trade but what he enjoyed most were the people he met.

"He made friends everywhere. They enriched his life, many became part of our very extended family. I learned so much about people and relationships from him. He helped me understand how unimportant material things are and how important people and our relationships with them are.

"It's only now, after he's gone, that I'm realizing what a profound gift he gave me and what a blessing he was in my life. He loved your columns in *Kentucky Living* because you write about people. His constant reminder to me was to come outside of myself and connect with people, to see life as an adventure and a journey.

"I believe that now he must be in Heaven, reunited with the storytelling friends who have gone before, saving a place at the table for those yet to come. He held a deep belief that death was not an end but was a beginning of a new adventure, a new journey.

"Sharing a little of his story with you has helped. How he's connected with one more person."

Letter for the Ages

Dear Great-Great-Great-Granddaughter/Grandson in the year 2105:

The reason for writing this open letter goes deeper and taller than symbols on a crumbled page or sounds chattering through October air.

We're writing about the dark, loamy circles on the slope in the southwest corner of our front yard here on Plum Lick where, in the autumn of 2005, there are two strong-minded stumps—all that's left of two Goliath water maples.

They were about eighty years old when a violent storm brought them down in the spring of 2001. We've studied it, and we figure the stumps might hold fast for another eighty years, give or take a decade.

These towering trees were two of ten saplings planted by the Prather family, about 1918, when they moved into this old house built by the brother of great grand-parent John Houston Crouch. That would have been, we calculate, about 1850.

Well now, as we write

from this vantage point stretching to you across to another new century, our main desire is for fresher remembrance and improved understanding—about water maples and people, like you and we. None of us wants to be forgotten!

Trees and human beings grow by each year adding another fresh round of cambium, which means they don't stay the same. They change every day and for that reason we'd no more top a tree and turn it into a bunch of sucker limbs than we'd tell a child you can only be "this much but no more."

Top a tree and you kill it. A tree doesn't deserve such a fate.

A child is no different. To discourage a child before he or she has grown is to design the same slow death.

One of the grandsons of these planters of trees, our neighbor Johnny Prather, puts it:

"Trees are like human beings. They're born and they ought to be able to live out their years until finally it's time to go."

Johnny greeted us at the door when we went to visit with him following his recent surgery, another operating room visit he holds in common with millions of mortals. We begin life by chance, live in the shadow of mounting medical bills, but do the best we can to grow as well as we dare to believe we can.

We know there're plenty of people who don't like water maples and write them off as trashy trees, but Johnny and we don't see it that way. There are all kinds of trees just as there all kinds of people. We don't mind root systems that go looking for new nourishment, and we don't curse the tree that slows down our mowing or might fall on our roofs. If we thought for one minute the tree in our yard had laid out a deliberate, mean-spirited strategy to crush us, we'd take down the tree or move to a place where there were no trees.

"That old hackberry out there." Johnny leans forward and points through the window. "When there was a story about 'the biggest hackberry in the state we went out there and measured ours and it was bigger than 'the biggest.' Why, that hackberry has to be two-hundred years old, at least."

Johnny was born more than seventy years ago in this same old Kentucky house where we now live and write. Once in awhile we feel inspired to reach out to future human saplings awaiting their turn to be born and grow. Johnny and we say, hang your swings high and sit in them as free as you can. Feel the breeze stirring beneath the seat of your pants and put a big smile on your face. Tighten your grip on the long ropes and ride the currents until you're filled with the glory of creation.

And don't forget to write a letter about it to your folks in 2205. You'll feel better for having done it, and they will too.

Kentucky–A State of Mind

We pray that this volume now resting in your hands will be an encouragement to read more, remember more, reflect more, and, maybe, to begin new journal keeping.

You are important!

As the years increase, we're grateful for each new day along the banks of Plum Lick Creek. God has seen fit to allow us to grow and prosper here.

We thank editors, Paul Wesslund and Anita Travis, of *Kentucky Living*, the rural electric cooperative magazine, and the widest circulated periodical in the Commonwealth of Kentucky. We are also grateful to editors Rachel Kamuf and Gary Huddleston, of Kentucky Farm Bureau's newspaper, *All Around Kentucky*, for their encouragement in the writing of many stories in *Kentucky—A State of Mind*.

We are grateful for the magic of our long-time illustrator and friend, Jackie Larkins, and for the patient skill of our graphic design artist, Stacey Freibert. Both have enriched the text.

The tales have been as true to life as we've been able to write them. Wherever there are mistakes, they are ours and no one else's.

In closing out this book, we're reminded of ninety-six-year-old Roscoe Cassidy, the whittler of cedar at Preston, in Bath County. It was he who when asked, what was his favorite knife, replied: "Boss."

Actually, the correct name is "Voss," a German company. Since we wanted to set the record straight, we called Helen Blevins, postmaster at Preston. She went out on the front porch, where Roscoe and the regular whittlers were busy making a new pile of shavings.

"What's the name of that knife, which you like so much?"

"Boss."

Another man seated nearby, quietly told Helen: "Voss."

The point is, nobody rushed in to correct anybody, the difference between a "B" and a "V" being such a small matter of differing speech. The larger issue is whether somebody has the good sense to be evenhanded more than heavy-handed.

When you're a Kentuckian, a whittler of cedar, a sustaining existence comes in the unfurling of the natural curl of life.

We follow in the footsteps of those whittlers at peace with themselves. You may find us in the flow of Plum Lick Creek on the way to the ocean, our destiny, and our hope for eternity.

It is well to remember, we do not sail alone. Our companions are those who share our belief that we are united in trust and respect in and for the good life, the state of mind we call home.